Nordic Nutrition

Eat Like A Viking

RHP & Hagen Wiking

DEDICATION

To our soon-to-be born son who will learn all what is written in this book.

CONTENTS

ACKNOWLEDGMENTS

A heartfelt thank you from both of us to Kim Nielsen, owner and author of the food blog Nordic Food and Living. He said yes to using his pictures in this book and it has visually taken this amalgamation of food, health, recipes, and culture to the next level!

INTRODUCTION

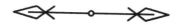

New Nordic Food has been a catchphrase for the last decade or so. It is hard to tell where it came from - perhaps the Nordic noir media subgenre of dark, realistic, and yet, uplifting tales. Or maybe it was the tire company who wanted to rate food - did it so well as to become the benchmark of the gastronomical world - calling it Michelin stars. Maybe they decided to check this New Nordic Cuisine out and ultimately rated these tire-stars for the first time as NOMA, or the abbreviation of "Nordisk Mad," Danish for 'Nordic Food.' Or perhaps it could even be the rise of Vikings and Norse mythology, partly due to the American TV show appropriately named "Vikings," as well as the Thor and Avengers movies.

Lastly, it could be, limited produce naturally grows in the cold variant of the temperate forest and lands, which Scandinavia calls home. With the arctic circle not being too far away. How it became popular is not the matter, just that it did, and that is why my wife and I decided to huddle up together to write this amalgamation of history, personal anecdotes, culture, nutrition, health, and recipe book. Combining my wife's proficiency in English, sporting it as her Native tongue and undying love of health, and my firsthand, living account as a Dane and understanding the history and stories around Scandinavian food and nutrition.

Food is undoubtedly a gateway into understanding a country's culture, history, and way of life. Slowly over many centuries, food can become the identity that defines a region. The historical perspective of food and anthropology is often a deep, rich story. Which, sadly, is unknown to many. It presents how geography defines the land and its people; through defining their food. But also, how those very same people told stories - myths -

legends about that very same food, and even in the naming of it tells the stories behind. By discovering this, you not only enrich the food you are eating - but you also discover hidden facets of a region that you always wanted to learn about. But never sat down to do so until now. Food provides fuel for you, but it also provides energy for the mind and soul. It is cliche, but it is true. And if you can do all this while being healthier, well, that is just a plain old bonus.

Being Danish, I have been mired in the Scandinavian food culture and health. While living abroad for years in multiple countries and having an American wife, I see the differences firsthand and how inspiration can be gained to achieve impactful benefits. Cultural inspiration and adoption, rather than appropriation.

Two concepts stand out when talking about Scandinavian culture, diet, and food-making: "langom" and "hygge." Langom translates to 'moderate' from Swedish and is about how everything should be done in moderation. Excess, consumerist craze, the broad strokes of me-personality, and stuffing ourselves with chemically enhanced dishes is not what langom is. It is a riff on the international "Slow Movement," not of actually being 'slow,' but to be selective in what you do, eat, and spend your precious time on. While doing these things, you savor them and get the most enjoyment out of them.

How this translates to food is not just in the ingredients that grow in the harsh northern soil. But also how it is moderately prepared. Seeing and tasting and feeling that the simplicity of foods actually enhances rather than degrades. When picking a few things to do and eat, you pick wisely and you pick these to be the highest of quality in your life. When doing this, you are not surrounded by mediocre things, food, and hobbies. You pick out from the most, that you care for the most, and bring you the most happiness. It is not a Minimalism book, but you may have heard variants of these sentences under this international design and lifestyle movement.

The next quintessential word and lifestyle guidance is "hygge," translating vaguely to 'pleasant togetherness.' Hygge can be seen on different levels. For one, it can be seen that being together with pleasant people that you love brings you happiness and contentment. But it is also about mutual trust. In Scandinavia, there is high trust between each other, strangers, or friends. People are still taken aback when I tell my friends from other countries that in Denmark, you leave your baby stroller outside the store - with your baby in it. This can be seen as 'hygge' and is so ingrained with food because more times than not hygge springs to life over a delicious array of people and meals.

2

The chapters are laid out in this order

First up is the Open-faced Sandwich, chapter one, which is all about the open-faced sandwich. We will dive into the history behind it and how versatile it is in the modern-day, going through toppings and ingredients. They are quick and healthy and will make you stand out anywhere. Basically transforming your lunch into a delicious health bomb.

When people hear the word "Viking," they think of a couple of things; horned helmets, large raiding brutes, and alcohol in the form of mead. Chapter two goes into the Norse mythology about mead and the effects it had on the Scandinavian people. It is surprisingly eye-opening and puts into perspective how little difference there was between a drunk Viking and a drunk you. This book shows you how to brew mead and how healthy it can be. Lastly, we will talk about mulled wine, or rather the Swedish Glögg. How it came to Sweden from a Southern empire and how Sweden took it and made it their own while linking it with the Christmas holiday in modern times. Then we will go into how to put it all together and how the health benefits connected to it are some of the best there are. A quick spoiler; the polyphenol, resveratrol - is the ultimate age-maximizing antioxidant.

Then we have Chapter three, which is all about Scandinavian porridge. Here we will highlight the dreary sadness of middle age porridge and the now trendy hipster-adored modern variant. Today it is loved as both breakfast, brunch, lunch, dinner, and dessert. Porridge is experiencing a rise due to its versatility and health. And is beginning to take hold outside of the northern, elongated nations, as well. Finishing it off with an equal part creepy and lovely Christmas tale. And how to make the cultural hallmark dish that is rice pudding or porridge.

Fresh ingredients and the act of foraging were a paramount part of our collective past. In some ways, the mindset of discovering food and being on the hunt picking greenery off the damp forest floor activates pleasure chemicals in our brain. But supermarkets, superstores, malls, and one-day shipping has turned us away from this enjoyable and fresh practice. But, not Scandinavia, or I should say, many Scandinavians compliment their grocery shopping with freshly picked, natural ingredients from the forest floor, riversides, beachline, and fields.

Chapter four is all about foraging. The act and culture of it. How to forage. But also, some of the most natural crops that were picked and the health benefits attached to them.

Chapter Five, smoked food, whether cold or hot, has always been an essential part of Nordic cuisine. We all have done it as farmer-herders, no matter where you were in the world. All before we found out we could jam freon inside of fridges and freezers to prolong the lifespan of food. This even led anthropologists to speculate that our brain is hardwired to enjoy smoked food, of which I certainly am a testimonial to that. This chapter goes into the art of the smoking technique, the history behind it, and how you can begin to smoke your own food from home.

Next up is chapter six and is the section of this book that many would directly link in their mind of what Scandinavia is known for, outside of the pivotal dishes of Swedish Meatballs and the Open-faced Sandwich. It is the sweets and pastries of the Scandi-lands. Why is it that northern Europe has such good pastries and cakes? I couldn't tell you, other than that high calories give you warmth, so maybe the weather has something to do with it. All these cakes and pastries tell of rich history and culture. You may be surprised at some of the traditional ingredients in these sweets, and how they are actually quite beneficial.

Chapter seven is "Cool Sea Divin'," and it does just that, dives under the sea. Scandinavia is cursed with a soil quality that is poorer than most regions in the world. Even weather that doesn't promote an abundance of crops. Because of this, the sea became part of everyday life for Scandinavians throughout history. It became both a source of food, but also a catalyst for mythology and living on the waves as second nature. The nutrition of seafood and algae will be especially focused on due to the very powerful and unique benefits for humans. You will see.

Then we have Chapter eight. Here we get into the northern meats and its raiding history. What made this standardized meat special in Scandinavia, and a slice of uncommon meat in Norway you might not have expected. It brings unique health benefits to the table and gives you some traditional recipes to test out.

Second to last is the bread and grains of Scandinavia - Chapter nine. And how the Vikings mythologized the energy and fiber-dense grain that is the rye. Then how this turned into hard-baked thin slices of rye bread and how this turned into the essential part of the open-faced sandwich; "smørrebrød". You will learn how to bake this bread yourself both as an old Norse and as modern-day bakeries do it in Scandinavia. All so it can give you the energy, so you can carry on the mythologization of this wonder-bread.

Last, but not least, we have chapter 10 with the Scandinavian garden. What grows there and how children are taught to cultivate their own produce. But also, the unique concept of 'Allotment Garden Huts.' The chapter goes into the berries, herbs, and grains that grow in Scandinavian soil organically. And the scientific facts behind the health and unique nutrition of such food.

*Figure 1 Pick a book, get it for **FREE**, and be signed up on our email list!*

Above - figure 1 - you will see both the catalog of books from both of us. If any of them strikes your fancy, then all you need to do is write an email to rhp.writer@outlook.dk with proof of purchase of this book, and then we will send you the **FREE** download link of the book you find interesting. Then you also get an email when each of us releases a new book, so you are the first to know.

Don't worry, we do not spam - we loathe spam emails myself.

Also, can we kindly ask you to leave a review of this book, telling the world what you liked or didn't like about this book. It really helps other people discover the book as well.

Thank   you,   and   we   sincerely   hope   you   will   enjoy   it!

GLOSSARY

ENGLISH	SWEDISH	NORWEGIAN	DANISH
RYE	RÅG	RUG	RUG
WHEAT	VETE	HVETE	HVEDE
BARLEY	KORN	BYGG	BYG
ONION	LÖK	LØK	LØG
SEA BUCKTHORN	HAVTORN	TINVED	HAVTORN
ROSEHIP	NYPON	ROSEHOFTE	HYBEN
ROSEHIP SOUP	NYPONSOPPA	-	-
ALLOTMENT GARDEN HUT	TILLDELNING TRÄDGÅRDSSTUGA	KOLONIHAGE	KOLONIHAVEHUS
BILBERRY	BLÅBÄR	BLÅBÆR	BLÅBÆR
LINGONBERRY	LINGON	TYTEBÆR	TYTTEBÆR
BEEF	NÖTKÖTT	STORFEKJØTT	OKSEKØD

ENGLISH	SWEDISH	NORWEGIAN	DANISH
DUCK	ANDA	ÅND	AND
PORK	GRISKÖTT	SVINEKJØTT	SVINEKØD
APPLE PORK	ÄPPELFLÄSK	-	-
DANISH RYE BREAD	-	-	RUGBRØD
REINDEER	REN	REINSDYR	RENSDYR
ROAST BEEF WITH VENISON SAUCE	-	DYRESTEK MED VILTSAUS	-
CHEESE DANISH	SEMLA	FASTELAVNSBOLLE	FASTELAVNSBOLLE
CHOCOLATE RYE BREAD BUN	-	-	CHOKOLADE RUGBRØDSBOLLE
RYE BREAD CHIPS	-	-	RUGBRØDSCHIPS
RED PORRIDGE WITH CREAM	-	-	RØDGRØD MED FLØDE
CROISSANT	-	KRUMKAKE	-
HONEY NUT CAKE	HONUNG NÖTKAKA	HØNNING NØTTEKAKE	HONNING NØDEKAGE
ALGAE	ALGER	ALGER	ALGER
KELP	KELP	TARE	TANG
OVEN-ROASTED COD WITH LEMON	UGNSSTEKT TORSK MED CITRON	OVNSSTEKT TORSK MED SITRON	OVNBRÆNDT TORSK MED CITRON

ENGLISH	SWEDISH	NORWEGIAN	DANISH
TOAST WITH PRAWNS/SHRIMP	TOAST SKAGEN	-	-
FISH MEATBALLS	FISK KÖTTBULLAR	FISK KJØTTBOLLER	FISKEFRIKADELLER
HARD BREAD	KNÄCKBRÖD	-	-
OPEN-FACED SANDWICH	-	-	SMØRREBRØD
STINGING NETTLE	BRÄNNÄSSLA	BRENNESLE	BRÆNDENÆLDE
ELDERBERRY	FLÄDERBÄR	HYLLEBÆR	HYLDEBÆR
MEAD	MJÖD	MJØD	MJØD
MULLED WINE	GLÖGG	GLØGG	GLØGG
RICE PORRIDGE	RISGRYNSGRÖT	RISGRØT	RISENGRØD

9

1

Having a public state-funded television channel as you have in most European countries, the Scandi ones included, brings up a lot of opinions from the public. Naturally, when you pay high taxes and pay through your salary to keep a tv station's lights on, you will want the content of said channel to jive with whatever disposition you see yourself having.

For you Americans out there: think of it this way. You have Netflix, but you didn't ask for or pay for Netflix, and yet here you are, having Netflix and also the payment exiting your bank account to have it, month after month. You cannot unsubscribe from Netflix, so you begin to have a lot of opinions if there is nothing on Netflix that you want to watch or if what is shown on Netflix is not something that you think is ethically right. This makes sense - and that is what many Scandi's feel like when it comes to their national television series of channels.

Okay, now take this feeling and multiply it with your children watching these shows you don't agree with, airing on this channel. This right here is what happened with the children's show in the late 1990s to early 2000s in Denmark for a show called "Anton min hemmelige ven," or 'Anton my secret friend.' It was a show about an adult who reminisces back on his childhood and his secret friend Anton going on hijinks together - tearing it up in the suburbs. Under this show's banner were segments where many angry parents speed-penned strongly worded letters of complaints to this national channel. One of these segments was named "Ulækre mad," or 'nasty food.' Here it was launch time and Sebastian, both the character in the show's and actor's actual name, had to get his afternoon open-faced sandwich or smørrebrød.

But rather than making something delicious, like the examples written later in this chapter, Sebastian, with his invisible friend Anton, made the nastiest open-faced sandwiches you can think of and consumed it. Foods mixing that of mackerel-tomato paste with strawberry jam, or chocolate with pickled beetroot and liver paste. Needless to say, Sebastian ate it all up, with children being thoroughly entertained and in many cases mirroring that of making these open-faced, nasty variants. Fervent complaints in letter format from parents occurred as they were upset about their trashed kitchens. And yes, my friends and I did make very nasty open-faced sandwiches when we were around 8 years old. [1]

This "smørrebrød" word with the strange symbols roughly means "buttered bread" or "open sandwich" in Danish, and it is a sandwich with a twist. If you happen to visit Denmark, you will see this fancy sandwich everywhere, but it's not what most would consider a normal sandwich. First of all, when you think of a sandwich you would think of some sort of white or wheat bread. Whether it is a multi- or single seed. But in Denmark, it is served on top of a thin but dense and strongly oven-roasted piece of dark rye bread, topped with meat or fish and plenty of veggies. If you're a Swede, you may recognize this as "smörgås," and "smørbrød" In Norwegian. But a typical Danish favorite to go to is smoked salmon or herring on top if an adult, and a simpler liver paste or pork sausage slices if a kid.

Scandinavian history is as long as it is interesting. Smørrebrød is said to date back to the 1800s when a quick, hearty lunch was essential during the workday. Workers would find as many toppings as they could and top it on some bread, stale or not, as a quick lunch recipe. This open-face sandwich idea is thought to date back even further. Ancient Vikings needed to preserve their food in the winter, and this was done by leaving bread and meat under the snow. In ancient times, stale bread was likely topped with lots of food, so the taste was masked, but they still received the calories of the bread. Today, it's not seen as a "struggle meal" as it was in the past, quite the contrary. It is a delicacy and there are many luxurious toppings, and they are sold for quite a few Kroners in Danish restaurants. Smørrebrød is gaining popularity in other countries and continents to this day, although most still aren't sure how to pronounce it. Danes have a grand time when asking foreigners to say this word!

I specifically have, as a kid, distinct memories of a primary school, this would be middle school in the US, a chiming bell signifying lunch-time. Every kid, girl, and boy opened up their daily backpack to unveil their luke-warm, and likely unsanitary, lunch box to get their liver paste and sliced Danish meatballs out. Toward my later years in school, I saw fridges being installed more and more with these lunch boxes being placed into them. I didn't read the news back then, but I imagine a health scandal came out that required the public school system to install these fridges for these questionable lunch boxes and their likely harboring of biological growth.

See "smørrebrød", is versatile in that it can be eaten for breakfast, lunch, dinner, or a snack - depending on what toppings you sport on them. It is an everyday meal, but in most cases, they are eaten as compliments to lunch when entering into the workplace in Denmark.

A traditional sandwich would have a piece of bread on top, however, this is an "open-faced" meal, with no bread on top. This is what makes it so popular and exclusive to Denmark. There are many variations of smørrebrød, and some of the ingredients and toppings include...

With all of these ingredients, a myriad of variants can be cooked up. In Denmark, the classics all come with a thin, strong oven-roasted slice of rye bread with butter smeared on top. Let's have a look at these different variants below:

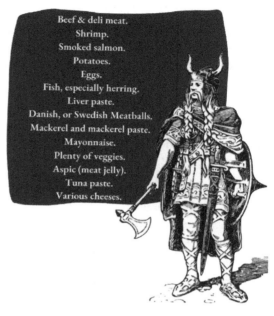

Beef & deli meat.
Shrimp.
Smoked salmon.
Potatoes.
Eggs.
Fish, especially herring.
Liver paste.
Danish, or Swedish Meatballs.
Mackerel and mackerel paste.
Mayonnaise.
Plenty of veggies.
Aspic (meat jelly).
Tuna paste.
Various cheeses.

Dyrlægens natmad.

Or the veterinarian's nightly food. This is one of the classics that most kids eat in their aforementioned lunchbox. Although, adults can also sneak one of these in as a snack to keep them going until dinner time. Dyrlægens natmad consists of liver pate with salted sliced ham on top, decorated with a bit of aspic, fresh onion rings, and cress. An interesting fact is that cress can actually be grown in damp cotton, rather than earthy soil. See in Denmark, in middle school, you have a plastic Tupperware-like box of which you fill this up with tons of cotton, as to create a solid rug of the white cotton-fluff floor. You would wet it with normal water, sprinkle the cress seeds on top, and lightly push the seeds down. You then go over to the sunny window frame and place the Tupperware-cotton-cress and wait. Over time these small cresses, grass-like herbs will begin to grow. Once it is fully grown you would take a scissor and cut some cress off for your dyrlægens natmad.

Leverpostejsmad.

Is next and it is with Liver pate with bacon and fried mushrooms. Whereas you also can add simple, pickled cucumber to make it a bit more layered.

Roast beef.
Then we have the one with the English name of "roast beef". This smørrebrød is thinly sliced roasted beef with some remoulade on top. A French paste made from mayonnaise used as a base. On top, you usually find shredded horseradish and fried onions.

Flæskestegsmad.
Next up we have "flæskestegsmad", the sliced roasted pork fashioned with boiled red cabbage and a slice of orange on top.

Rullepølsemad.
2 to 3 slices from a sausage roll, decorated with raw onions and sliced tomatoes. This one is a particular favorite in the aforementioned kid's lunch box, although not for one's nostrils.

Røget laksemad.
Or smoked fresh salmon slices, although this time it is not the hard roasted rye bread but light and fluffy wheat bread. Then you sprinkle some fresh shrimp on there and some mayo, and you may want to add a slice of citrus on there as well.

Æg og rejemad.
Next up we have "æg og rejemad", which is an either hard or soft boiled egg with fresh shrimp, cress, and mayo. So to not become too dry.

Stjerneskudsmad.
This one can also be a variant in a cocktail glass if at a fish specialized restaurant, but in its open-faced sandwich variant, it is a slice of toasted light wheat bread, a white plaice fish on one end, and then a breaded plaice on the other. On top, you will find fresh shrimp, with mayo, cucumber salad, caviar, beetle roe, or small fish eggs, and a lemon slice to give it a fresh touch. Quite the tour around the watery depths.

Sol over Gudhjem.
Then we have "Sol over Gudhjem", which is directly translated to 'sunlit Gudhjem, or sun over Gudhjem'. Gudhjem is a picturesque and idyllic old

fishing hamlet on the Danish island of Bornholm. The fishing hamlets littered around this rocky island were and still are known for their fishing and smoking of said fish. As you will read all about in the "Smokin' Hot" chapter below. Naturally, the central tasting element in this open-faced sandwich is smoked fish, which is smoked herring slices, added with raw onions and chives. Some even like to put some radishes on there and raw egg yolk.

Pariserbøffemad.

Next up we have another variant that harbors its name from a place in the world, but this place you have most definitely heard about. It is called "pariserbøffemad", and is translated to 'Paris beef food'. Nobody knows why this one is related to Paris, because when I begin to describe it in a few words you will see that it matches more to America due to its hamburger meat. You start with roasting a light wheat bread slice in butter on your pan, then you put a fried hamburger patty on it, place some fresh or roasted onions on there as well. And top it off with egg yolk, pickles, shredded horseradish, red beets, and hijackers.

Kartoffelmad.

The last one is also the simplest and is "kartoffelmad" or 'potato food'. Of which the lovingly joking potato-Danes will escape the mouths of both Norwegians and Swedes when they link any potato-related food or vegetable with Danes. Why? Because the Danish language in its dialect and pronunciation is very different from that of Norwegian and Swedish. Up until the writing of this book, one solid answer from linguists hasn't been found as to why. But Danes when they speak will sound very guttural as if they have a potato in their throat, although they still sound Germanic and Norse, so many Scandinavian words will be similar. It is funny though and hence why there is the potato-Dane joke. This smørrebrød is made with sliced, freshly boiled potatoes, fashioned with raw onion slices and spicy mayo - sometimes with bacon on top as well.

These combinations make it a perfectly balanced meal, high in protein, fiber, and Omega 3's and 6's if there is seafood on top. Shrimp and other seafood have anti-inflammatory and anti-aging properties while also being extremely heart-healthy. The calories and fat in seafood are low while the nutrition is dense. Rye bread is full of natural fiber, which of course keeps you full for longer, which aids weight loss. The Scandinavian' love for rye bread may be a contributing factor in their low obesity and diabetes rates. Rye comes packed full with antioxidants, and a full panel of vitamins and minerals. Smørrebrød is essentially a guilt-free, yet super satisfying meal.

2

MEAD AND MULLED WINE

The northern lands vary widely when it comes to a propensity for intoxicating liquors. While the US went through a well-intentioned but idealistically blind prohibition, so too did Sweden, called the Bratt system, and Norway as well. But it never happened in Denmark, so alcohol is central to the culture - for better or worse. This means that there is a great difference between Denmark and the two other Scandinavian countries. For example, there is a friendly running joke in Denmark that many Swedes travel down south to Denmark only to buy alcohol to then leave again. We have many jokes running between each other in all four sibling countries.

The point is that growing up in Denmark, you get an inherent unhealthy relationship with alcohol that then is normalized upon gaining the wisdom of adulthood and enough bad "days after." It is no joke that the average Danish teen drinks about double the alcohol consumption compared to the European average and amounts to some of the very highest drinkers in the world. [2] Almost repeatedly, year by year, you will read a news article that the Bulgarian government is rather perturbed with the damage Danish youth leave in their wake while being on their alcoholic-bender during the warm summer months called "Sunny Beach."

But this cultural, modern-day stance for alcohol traces back to history.

The History of mead

Contrary to popular belief, mead is actually thought to be invented by the Chinese in the 7th millennium BCE. While, much later, in Greek mythology, it is construed that mead was called "the drink of the Gods". [3]

Figure 2 A Norse mythology image from the 18th century Icelandic manuscript "SÁM 66", now in the care of the Árni Magnússon Institute in Iceland, Public Domain

But if you would travel back in time to ask a Norsemen where this horned drink came from, they would say...

In the world of the cold Viking north, the Gods didn't much like each other. Or rather, some really didn't like each other, and others just tolerated one another. In a lot of ways, the old Sagas resemble that of old family rivalries and squalls. One day, one of the family squabbles went too far as to need an intervention. This surprised-you-did-something-wrong event was when two warring tribes of Gods came together to agree that they all indeed did something wrong. Their ritual for an agreement was to all spit in a bowl.

But from this vast collection of God spit sprang forth Kvasir - the wisest of them all. Kvasir was in general living it up, quite content to have parents in the number of tens: created from spit. But one day, in Kvasir's singing and storytelling stupor, he was the guest of two very impolite and inhospitable dwarves; Fjalar and Galar. Dwarves in Norse Mythology were considered great builders and craftspeople. So rather than starting the dinner party, they killed Kvasir and turned his blood into what is known as "Mead of Poetry." Eventually, this poetic drink landed in the hands of a giant, of which Odin was quite displeased that the giant would have all the fun. Odin went to the giant's lair, seduced the giant's wife with his godly charms, turned into an eagle, downed all of the mead, and flew away. [4] Then eagle-Odin flew over to many jars and urns and barrels to spit all of the Kvasir-liquid into them. See above in figure 2 to get a visual.

This eagle relief became known that when anyone drank it they would turn into skalds and scholars. This is kind of interesting because when you or I have a grand old time with some drinks, we get a wee bit overwhelmed, either turning into singers (mostly not great) or dramatic storytellers or boastful in our vast knowledge about everything; able to answer any question, ever. Alcohol had the same effect on the raiders, and I guess the Vikings created a mythic tale to signify a good night out.

Another interesting fact about mead is that another legend tells of when warriors fall in battle they get sent to Norse heaven - Valhalla. Where, upon arriving, they get handed a draught of mead from many maidens around. This legend over time turned into that in Scandinavia newlywed married people are handed 28 days - or one lunar cycle - worth of mead to keep them going. As we will learn below, mead was made from freshly cultivated honey, and the lunar cycle turned into the name "honeymoon". A moon's worth of Mead from honey. This old concept is where the English-speaking world got the word "honeymoon" from. An etymological history of godly spit and two inhospitable dwarves.

The Vikings, therefore, enjoyed a strong alcoholic drink during celebrations and festivals. Mead, in Danish and Norwegian is "mjød", and "mjön" in Swedish. This is one of the oldest alcoholic drinks in history, even older than ale or wine. So what is it exactly? It is a fermented drink made from water and honey, and sometimes with added spices or sweet fruits. What makes it an alcoholic drink is the fermented sugar that is released from the honey. Another big misconception to popular belief was that Vikings constantly drank mead. Yes, they did bottom copious amounts of dizzying ambrosia. But mead was preserved for special occasions and for royalty, not so much as a common drink. [5] Although they did drink enough to get the surprising benefits.

The health benefits of mead

While mead itself is not considered healthy, the Welsh physician Meddyglyn may begin to dispute one's claims. See mead became healthy due to the flavoring herbs and spices that were added, such as cloves, ginger, rosemary, and thyme. Sometimes grains would be added to speed up fermentation. [6]

Because of this central honey element, this dizzying drink has also been called "honey wine". And this is where we find the actual health benefits connected to standard mead, while the fermentation process itself has bacterial cultures in the drink that aid your digestion and gut health as a probiotic.

See honey itself has been used as a medicinal remedy for us humans for millennia, where today it is proven to have antioxidant and antimicrobial benefits. Essentially, honey aids the protection and strengthens your cells' natural defenses, which comes with its own vast health and wellbeing benefits. [7] This is why today we will make a loved one a nice cup of tea with honey in it if they have a sore throat. The antibacterial properties and antioxidative properties soothe your throat and makes it bearable to eat and drink. In some dietary and herbalist circles, it is believed that mead, with its fermented honey, contains these benefits. But more evidence to show this is needed to say for sure.

Mead acts as a probiotic. See probiotics, as it is called, can directly be bought as a supplement and has been taking off in health circles for years. For a long time, many have outright neglected one's gut and subsequent gut health. This is strange if you think about it since it is your gut that secondarily accepts foreign elements into your body to break it down. The first one being your mouth, which is its own bacterial culture. Probiotic strains take about 30 minutes before a meal aids digestion, and the extraction of nutrients and breaking down of harmful stuff from your food. It is, therefore, a blanket solution and should be on anybody's radar when designing one's supplements cupboard or dietary plan. Because through this, by having a healthy gut, you will have a stronger immune system in general. Even research is beginning to show that probiotic strains lead to the prevention and treatment of chronic complications such as cancer, allergies, heart disease, and gastrointestinal disorders, such as gastroparesis. [8,9]

Overall mead is not that popular of a drink and is therefore also linked with the limited amount of research put into it. Our scientific world is linked with our economy, or our collective actions, so we know an insurmountable amount of the benefits and side-effects of coffee for example. But none with the benefits or side-effects of mead. But as a direction here, it could be that the varying added spices and herbs to mead can affect, aid, or counteract the honey and fermented probiotic strains in mead. While the same can be said about the alcoholic element, which in mead varies between 5% to 20% at its strongest. [10] In conclusion, as it is with all alcoholic beverages, it should be consumed with caution. Wine is known to hold jaw-dropping benefits, but it is an alcoholic beverage so it should be consumed with care. We don't know for sure if mead has those same benefits, even though our past you and me seems to disagree, so for now, mead should be consumed for pleasure. So here is how it is made.

Figure 3 Honey Fruit Mead Brewing by Evan-Amos, Public Domain

How mead is made

First off, you will need 2 to 3 pounds - 500 grams to 1 kilogram - of honey (if you can, organic and fresh), distilled or filtered water, and a bit of yeast, 2 grams or a half of a teaspoon.

1. Heat 0.5 gallons - or 2.7 liters - of water up, so it simmers.

2. Then add your honey, 2 pounds - 500 grams - to make a "dry" tasting mead, or 3 pounds - 1 kilogram - to make a "sweet" tasting mead. Stir around the honey until it is fully dissolved.

3. Let it then simmer for 30 minutes, removing any scum that has formed. Take it off the heat and cool it down to around 100 Fahrenheit - 37/38 Celsius. Then grab it and pour it into a glass container or jar.

4. Now you can add any herbs or spices that you think you would like, traditional mead didn't add any of these. But over time mead was made with many interesting flavors such as ginger, thyme, lemon, or fruit.

5. Check the temperature consistently with a thermometer when your mead has hit 90 degrees Fahrenheit - 32 Celsius - add the yeast. The amount of yeast depends on how much mead you are making. Use around 2 grams - half a teaspoon - of yeast.

6. Close the glass lid, either it being a jar or a container of some sort, and begin to shake your mead well - the more the better. Add a bit of water until the mead is a few inches - 5 centimeters - from the top. Then place an airlock on top as opposed to your lid, you can search for it online, they are inexpensive.

7. Place the bottle in a cold and dark place and let it just fester there for about 6 weeks. Good mead is a waiting game. Tip: if you add any fruits or sugary herbs or spices bubbles will start to form within 12 to 24 hours which will get trapped in the airlock. Simply just clean the airlock and place it on the mead again. Check it occasionally, after weeks you should see the bubbling grind to a slow pace. Approximately one bubble every minute or so. Once that is the case and you have hit close to the 6 weeks mark, see above figure 3, then it is time to bottle it and enjoy it chilled.

As mentioned, alcohol is a two-headed beast. One will bite your hand, the other would like to be your pet. Alcohol, consumed responsibly can yield strong results and benefits, but too much and it becomes a light poison. The same is the case with wine.

Mulled wine's Scandinavian variant of Glögg and its history

Usually, when we think of vast spanning empires and conquering nations we think of them in a bad light. Much of this is within reason, empires like the Roman empire, killed not just people but also languages, traditions, and even whole cultures. In Spain, many languages died out for a central Latin-rooted equivalent. This is a destruction of cultural heritage and is not good, but it also unified the world. While many of the technological advancements of the Roman empire were introduced to other nations not sporting an aqueduct water system or sewers. The Roman empire has left in its fall still far-spanning effects on history, even up until today. For example, the metropolis and financial center of the world, London, and debatably the British empire, wouldn't have existed if it wasn't for the Roman empire. But outside of financial centers and a global language being English and Latin-based ones like Spanish, the Roman legions also brought with them mulled wine.

Mulled wine was discovered in Greece, by a figure we have spoken about before, Hippocrates - the Father of Medicine. See mulled wine with its honey and spices was considered an ailment for sickness. Mirroring in a lot of ways how mead came to be. Side note: it is interesting how mulled wine, or in Scandinavia "Glögg or Gløgg" became a household cultural beverage consumed during the Christmas 'hygge'. But the Northern European and Nordic equivalent mead has overall died out in consumption in Scandinavia today - outside of specialist breweries and blonde hipsters. Back to history. The Roman empire spread mulled wine far to distant lands, eventually also landing in the places that the Roman legions never reached; Scandinavia - Sweden. But while mulled wine fizzled out over the years after the fall of the Roman empire, new variants sprang forth in each country around Europe during the Medieval age. Sweden was no different and made theirs with milk, spices, and wine named Lutendrank. Later on, during the 1800s, Lutendrank turned into Glögg and was connected to Christmas. [11] It became a staple in Sweden, and through Sweden, this grew to Norway and Denmark. Now, Glögg is commonplace in any Scandinavian household during December. There do exist many similarities between mulled wine and Glögg, however, there are some central differences. We will get to those, but first, let's look over the miraculous benefits linked with warmed spiced wine.

Health benefits of Glögg

To talk about the health benefits of Glögg is to talk about wine; or more telling, grapes.
In health circles wine, or grapes, are lauded as one of the wonder-drinks to fight diseases, boost overall health, and even increase your lifespan through DNA repair and inert cell cleanup - a blood cleaner. Yup, you heard that right - wine is an alcoholic drink that is anti-aging. A real-life mythical vitality drink.

The contributor to this is the two polyphenols called resveratrol and fisetin which are found in the skin of the grape.
Resveratrol does this by damaging your cells so your body gets provoked to repair your cells naturally. This sounds bad, but is actually very effective and outright repairs your cell's DNA, fat disbursement, glucose and insulin output, inflammation healing; so internal damage, and nervous system repair. While fisetin is the other polyphenol that does not damage your cells but actually cleans up your inert or dead cells that still float around in your bloodstream. This medically is called anti-senescence. See as we age our natural processes get worse at dispelling these dead cells just going around your body, this is partially what makes us age. Fisetin, the polyphenol found in grapes and thereby wine - Glögg - directly goes in and helps our body clean out these inert cells. [12]

Back to resveratrol.
So for the cells which are alive, the DNA in every cell is its programming or brain. If there is something malfunctioning in our DNA, our cells themselves act against our body's favor and health. Over time, our DNA is damaged and needs repair. But as we age, it is harder for our body to repair our DNA naturally. Resveratrol directly aids this process naturally and is therefore considered to be anti-aging. In mice, resveratrol and the natural function in our body that repairs cell DNA called sirtuin saw an increase in life-span by 16% in females and 9% in males. That is an average translated to human years of 12.5 years for women and 7 years for men. Now to make something clear, this is not to say that resveratrol and fisetin extend lifespan. It just maximizes lifespan, so it gets the most out of your body as possible - which on average translates to these years.

But in the ambrosia lies a fly.
Because you can take too much which gives your cells too much stress

and damage and then needs too much DNA repair. All in all, having an adverse effect - doing more harm than good. See it a bit as a controlled burn. A forest that can grow too wildly with too many invasive species can be burned away artificially by humans. By doing that, you free up and activate the natural biomes within forests themselves to repair and start from scratch. But burning the forest too much will either permanently damage the forest or there is no forest any longer whatsoever. So, take Glögg or grapes or wine in moderation, and it will extend how long you will live. Personally, I eat grapes every other day or drink 1 glass of red wine. Or in December, Glögg, every other day. Likewise, I only take the resveratrol supplement on relaxing days; not on days, I work out. Because overly stressing your body and subsequent cells will do more harm than good. [13–16] So this is with mulled wine in general, but as we have gone through the cultural Scandinavian Christmas drink of Glögg, it is slightly different with fillings of almonds and raisins, while being spiced with cardamom, clove, and ginger - sometimes with sliced oranges floating around in your Christmas mug. Let's start with almonds and raisins.

As the saying goes, 'all the nutrients are located in the skin.' Well in almonds case, that is true. Because the brown skin layer of almonds is where all the delightful antioxidants are located. Which by now, you should get a reminder of what they do to your cells inside of your body, just remember that the benefits are anticancer and anti-aging. Likewise, almonds are one of the best methods to get vitamin E, with the "vitamin" -the name being a bit misleading as it is actually another type of antioxidant. The name aside, what vitamin E does is to hatch itself to the protective wall or membrane around each of your cells making them withstand oxidation more and thereby making your cells work for longer for you. Lastly, almonds with their high amount of protein and fiber help to regulate your blood sugar levels. So people with type-2 diabetes should get a good dose of almonds every day. [17] Raisins, being just sundried grapes should contain the same amount of benefits as grapes - at least that is what logic would tell us. Well, this is not the case. And is a good thing, because then getting your Glögg then will cover the whole gamut of health you need. In short, raisins are excellent for boosting your iron levels. So if you are prone to fainting, then eat some raisins. Raisins can also help you with digesting food and keeping your bone structure strong. While raisins do hold a dense level of calories, even more than soda. They are, therefore, sometimes used by athletes as a source of calories and energy. [18] At last, raisins were even found to aid your oral health and fight against cavities. This is because raisins contain phytochemicals that directly fight bacteria in your mouth. And good oral health is linked to a reduction in you getting heart, or cardiovascular disease, it overall protects your brain cells, decreases the risk of kidney disease, and decreases cancer risks. To top it off, if you are a woman and are trying to get pregnant, or even currently are pregnant, then good oral hygiene is linked to stronger fertility and overall healthier pregnancies. [19,20]

Next, we have the spices that make mulled wine into Glögg; cardamom, clove, and ginger. In an experiment using mice, these little critters were given cardamom powder. Which resulted in the mice promoting their own natural increase of enzymes that fight cancer in their body. Here scientists injected skin cancer cells into two groups of mice. One group got cardamom powder and the other group didn't. 12 weeks later the experimenters noted that only 29% of the group of mice that got cardamom developed skin cancer, whereas the other group 90% of the mice developed skin cancer. Likewise, it has been found that cardamom also increases the body's natural ability to attack existing cancer, called 'killer cells'. [21–23] We have even tested this on human cells but lab results of which have yielded similar results. [24] Although, further and more specific testing on actual living humans needs to be carried out. Furthermore, if you struggle with stomach ulcers or sores on your stomach floor from a certain bacterial disease or too much aspirin, cardamom was found to actually be better at fighting these ulcers than lab-made anti-ulcer medication. [25] Concludingly, cardamom also has been found to improve breathing disabilities since cardamom's essential oil extracts, when inhaled, have been found to increase oxygen consumption significantly. Both helpful for asthmatics and athletes alike. [26] Cardamom and clove are both considered great in protecting your liver and making it function at its best. [27–29]

The last to shine a spotlight on is ginger. And if you, like me, grew up in Denmark and experienced in your unruly teen years that ginger is very effective at lessening nausea after a bender, after all those Sunday mornings after. But discounting the cultural fixation of alcohol in Denmark, ginger is also used as a nausea ailment in the treatment of chemotherapy for cancer patients. [30–32] While ginger also is used commonly for pregnant women in their morning, midday, afternoon, and evening sickness. But if you are pregnant consult your doctor if you should supplement with ginger since it has been known to cause blood clots, something pregnant women already are at higher risk for. One of the main complications that come with age, which also has a genetic component, is joint pain and stiffness. Fortunately, ginger is proven to help with the pain and even with the flexibility that is being lessened. Staying on the pain topic; ginger is a known supplement to take in pain relief against menstrual pains. It was even found that it was just as effective as a medicinal pain reliever, such as ibuprofen. [33–35]

Glögg

1 bottle of red wine.

Half a cup of sugar.

2 tablespoons of orange zest.

Likewise, 2 tablespoons of raisins.

1 tablespoon cardamom.

2 tablespoons of chopped ginger root.

1 cinnamon stick.

8 cloves.

2 tablespoons of almonds.

And then some orange slices.

Glögg differs from mulled wine in two aspects: the fillings put into it, and the spices used.

When living in Scandinavia you can buy pre-mixed fillings for Glögg, but having lived, and currently living, abroad I found out that this pre-mix doesn't exist. So you'll have to buy it separately.

Serves: 2-3

Prep time: 5-10 Minutes

3

THE RENEWAL OF PORRIDGE

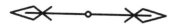

When you think of the word 'porridge,' an image most likely comes to your mind. Maybe there are shivering men in a dark, musty-smelling tavern. Or an image of Scandinavians in the cold, dark, and unforgiving winter, eating a very basic bowl of sloppy lukewarm oat porridge. Or you possibly think of the modern version. Which is typically just porridge with a bit of butter, and maybe cinnamon - if you are feeling extra daring. And you would be correct either way. Since the Viking age, and likely prior, porridge (aka grød in Danish, gröt in Swedish, and grøt in Norwegian) was the go-to for most meals. The first record of oat porridge being mentioned was sometime in the 14th century in Scandinavia. Grains and porridge were the normal diets of these ancient conquerors. In these times, breakfast, lunch, and dinner typically had some sort of porridge in it. It was quick, easy, and very filling. Porridge was quite popular in Scandinavia. This was since only a small amount of certain grains can grow in the harsh cold climate, namely oats and barley. Wheat and rye could also grow, but not as often or as easily as the barley and oats. The Vikings made use of what was available and took what they could get, and made porridge as often as they could.

Traditionally, porridge was very simple to make, being that there was no kitchen available. The only ingredient was usually just water, grains, and salt. It was meant to be a no-nonsense type of meal.

To add flair and flavor to the mushy and often bland taste, they would add berries, fruit, herbs, and veggies to this dish.

While oat porridge may not always be the most delicious in flavor, it sure does pack a nutritional punch. As mentioned before, this is what these ancient, powerful Norsemen lived off of. Let us take a look at the benefits. While grød does have quite a bit of carbs, don't let that deter you just yet! When we think of oats, most instantly will think of healthy fiber, and that's exactly what porridge is chock full of. Fiber not only keeps you fuller for longer, but it also helps to regulate your bowel movements and prevents constipation. Who could fight a Viking battle while constipated anyway? The benefits go deeper than that, however. You can thank fiber for reducing the risk of diabetes, heart disease, high blood pressure, obesity, and certain cancers.

Oats contain a very special compound strictly found only in plants and grains, and this is called polyphenols. So what is a polyphenol and what makes it so beneficial? Polyphenols are most commonly found in foods such as nuts, berries, spices, and herbs. There are actually over 5,000 different types of polyphenols, but we won't go over all of them. The main reason why they are so beneficial is that they are a powerhouse of antioxidants. Antioxidants are essentially anti-disease compounds that protect our whole body. Studies have shown that those who eat a diet high in polyphenols have a much longer lifespan than those who do not. This is because they lower your risk for diabetes, cancer, and heart disease just to name a few. Heart disease is one of the highest killers of citizens in the United States, and it is not spoken about enough. These 3 conditions collectively are the highest-ranking diseases in the U.S. Polyphenols also slow down aging, and help fight viral and bacterial infections in our body. But the most unbelievable part is not yet spoken about enough. Polyphenols have been proven in many studies to *kill* cancer cells, making it a very interesting topic for scientists and nutritionists. This is what makes porridge a superfood and could have likely contributed to the strength shown by the ancient Vikings.

Now let us look at which vitamins and minerals are also in the average bowl of porridge…

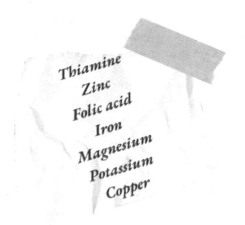

Thiamine
Zinc
Folic acid
Iron
Magnesium
Potassium
Copper

Who needs a multivitamin when there is "grød"?

The traditional Scandinavian way of preparing porridge is painfully simple. You would need 2 ingredients. Water and oats, nothing else. But it was what was added to it that made it bearable for the palate and so versatile. The Scandinavians had a cauldron over a fire and would simply add their oats or barley - then add water. It was then simmered until the consistency was thick like a paste. As mentioned before, berries, herbs, veggies, and fruit were added to make it more flavorful. This was a filling meal that nearly every Scandinavian family ate, not just for the poor or rich. They had to eat what was vastly available and what was easily cooked. And not much has changed since those times. Modern Scandinavians are finding their love again for porridge, and many porridge-only restaurants, appropriately named "Grød" are open and thriving. Nowadays, the variety of porridge is vast and tempting, with breakfast, lunch, and dinner options available. This is an "updated" version from just oats and water bland porridge. It is no more. It's incredible that thousands of years later, this dish is still widely consumed. Let's have a look.

Some common toppings and fillings for modern porridge include...

BREAKFAST

Skyr (Icelandic yogurt).

Fruit (such as berries, acai, mango, apples, bananas).

Peanut/Almond Butter.

Jam (such as strawberry, raspberry, blackberry).

Granola.

Seeds (such as chia, hemp, or sesame).

Rhubarb.

Coconut flakes.

Banana.

Nuts (such as almonds, hazelnuts, or peanuts).

Honey.

Sweet toppings such as chocolate, Nutella, or jam

LUNCH & DINNER

Mushrooms.

Cabbage.

Risotto.

Peppers.

Onions.

Tomatoes.

Asparagus.

Cheese (such as Parmesan, mozzarella, or cheddar).

Various herbs and spices

The history and custom around the Christmas rice porridge

"Risengrød" is a dish and Christmas tradition that is well known and well-loved in Denmark. If you are Danish, you will know this well and likely have fond memories. Traditional porridge is used with water, but not with this special dish. Served on Christmas or Christmas Eve, risengrød is made with milk or cream, butter, and cinnamon. This little upgrade was for good reason, and it all starts with a little Christmas legend.

Every little kid, when stopped doing their rumpus and asked about their favorite time of year, will immediately respond with "Chrithmath!" And quickly move on with their rumpus.

I was no different growing up in Denmark. But one of my distinct memories that my family had was recreating an age-old Christmas legend and popular Christmas jingle.

A tale and song about kindness and empathy of the magically unseen. The encapsulation of what the ideal Christmas spirit was.

Every December morning, my brother and I would, in our morning stupor, take our chocolate-filled rectangle box always placed disorderly at the end of our dinner table. We knew which box was which because we each wanted different depictions on our chocolate square. I was more into the snowscapes of nature and a small village, and my brother gravitated towards a shoulder-height view of happen-stances inside of big towns. On each box, 24 closed paper-gates were littered throughout this either landscape or town scene - each gate guarding a piece of milk chocolate in the shape of a Christmas critter, reindeer, or Santa himself. Every kid in Denmark would take this box, every morning, and count the days with chocolate and a small tale being told on the inside of this chocolate-bouncer-gate now opened, day-by-day until it was the 24th of December - yes, Americans and Brits, Christmas is celebrated the 24th in Denmark. On most of these days, after finishing up the homemade Christmas-themed ornamental girandole, to have yet another method of counting down the countdown to the great gift day in the form of a candle, you would boil up some "risengrød," or Rice/Christmas porridge. There were four in my family so we each received a portion with a spoon of butter and cinnamon. But even though we were four, we created five portions.

See, you always would leave a portion for your friendly-attic-gnome. A creature of old greying age, about knee-height, rocking a red hat with a white puff-ball on top, impossibly red cheeks, and an unstoppable hunger for the rice-butter-cinnamon mix. Otherwise, the gnome would begin to move things around in a playful manner and make teasing noises - fun, lighthearted stuff. In hindsight, it is only slightly terrifying. My family, of course, did this and went up to the attic to place the bowl; feeding the imaginary gnome. And if your parents wanted to keep up the ruse, they would dump the now slightly spoiled porridge the morning after to say that the gnome had slurped it all up. This was always followed by impossibly big, amazed kid-eyes and an insistence on doing it again.

Figure 4 Lundby nissen 1842 by Johan Thomas Lundbye, Public Domain

Upon looking into the roots of this custom, you travel back in time all the way to the Viking age. Here the gnome – see figure 4 - wasn't just a nondescript gnome - it was a farm-gnome. Usually residing not in the house attic, but in the barn's loft. During winter, where produce was scarce, and food stores had to be protected from desperate hungry wolves and bears,

Vikings believed that this farm-elf would protect their food. These small magical imps - gnomes - leprechauns - trolls were worshipped as an idol of lesser godly beings living amongst us.

As Else Marie Kofod, an expert in Danish folk songs says, in Danish, but translated here, about these lactose-happy red cheeks being a home-protector. But-but, they wouldn't perform without some gruel offering, "... if you would please this elf, then they needed something to eat. Back then you didn't have rice, so you instead made sweet porridge made from overboiled grain in sweetened milk. That then was placed close to the elf, even sometimes with a clot of butter on top. We can therefore deduce that this meal, back then, was considered a form of ritualistic/party meal." [36]

But what differed from back then was that it wasn't a Christmas season ritual - this was done year-round. It was essentially seen as your own little house-elf, like the Harry Potter Dobby. Although, as opposed to a magical realism book series for children and later young adults, this farm-elf could be mean-spirited. See, if you didn't please your farm-protector, then they would do just a little bit more than just teasing. You could come into your barn accompanied by your eye-morning-crust at the crack-jack of dawn to get your daily milk and upon seeing your cow Maisy - you would see that her head has been turned 180 degrees - lifeless on the barn floor. Quite dark - but if you read any of the old Norse Sagas, then you know it can be pretty grim.

After the Pagan beginnings of ritualistic offerings, the upper crusts of Denmark caught wind of this colorful past and decided to make it a bit posher. The cultural subset of the aristocracy in Denmark began to see a more peaceful potential for the gnome. Because in 1813 Denmark had just lost their dominant military fleet in Europe during the Napoleonic wars and, as a result, had gone broke nationally. To strengthen the national identity the Danish cultural elite looked for every opportunity to find more lighthearted tales to tighten the struggling family life in Denmark. They wanted to transform the scary gnomes into Christmas gnomes with a friendlier disposition and less murdering of pasture animals. See, what is known today as Christmas Day and Eve was developed during this time and came from other countries' Christmas traditions that were taken to heart. But something needed to be rooted in Danish history and folklore, so they took these animal murdering imps and made them nice, enchanting, and kid-friendly. [37]

How to make Christmas-themed rice pudding

So to not get on the bad side of the little Christmas imps, it is pretty clear that you need to learn how to make fresh rice pudding, or porridge, with cinnamon and butter. Well, you are in luck. It is very easy, tastes delicious, and keeps the enchanting imp away. And this book will show you just how to do this. First, you will need…

What you need

1/3 cup or 3 fl oz of chilled water.

1/2 cup or 5 grams of porridge-friendly rice.

3.5 cups or 35 fl oz of fresh, chilled sweetened milk.

1 pinch of salt.

How to make

Place the water & rice in a pot and bring it to a boil for 2 minutes.

Add the sweetened milk & bring to a boil, while stirring. This breaks down the rice which creates the noticeable substance of porridge or pudding. Boil for 1 hour, this will let the broken down rice turn into one cohesive substance. Add a pinch of salt.

Once done, take out your most beautiful bowl, make a serving, with a clot of butter in the middle slowly melting from the warm pudding, & add cinnamon powder all over.

SERVES: 1-2
COOKING TIME: 1 HOUR

4

WHAT LURKS IN THE FOREST

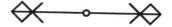

In many schools littered through the three Scandinavian countries, the proximity to forests is close. This has prompted the primary schools of the Scandinavian lands to frequently visit the local woods to learn about what lurks within.

No trolls are found, but plenty of mushrooms, moss, and trees are around. With usually a guide of some sort. Either in the living form of a biologist knowing a lot about the cold temperate plants or an accompanying booklet with added questions for the younglings. The main point is that I vividly remember going to the biggest forest loosely connected with Copenhagen; "Hareskoven", and "Jonstrup Skov", multiple times a year to document the change of life with the seasons of the same plants and living beings adapting to a light, gentle frizzle moving to a mean snowy blizzard.

In essence, many Scandinavian families take pride in going to the forest to forage. Finding edible mushrooms, picking pesky stinging nettle, even in some cases sapping some sticky, sweet tree sap. The act of going to the forest for one makes you more aware, intelligent, and kinder - actual science [38,39] - and two, centers you and makes you aware of the seasons changing and how we as humans are connected to the land in wondrous ways. You essentially achieve a deeper connection to your surroundings. But also in extension, to yourself and with what you eat.

When it comes to foraging, be very mindful of what you pick up off the ground. Or scavenge from that bush or plant before you eat or make it into a dish. Plants, herbs, berries, mushrooms, chanterelles, and grasses have this annoying habit of looking very much alike. So either consult a very descriptive book, this one **not** included, or have a similar aforementioned, living biologist on your tail to quarterback sack you to the mossy dirt before you eat something poisonous.

Check the laws about foraging in your country. In the Scandinavian countries, it is legal. Just as a quick example, we have in Sweden the law called "Allemansrätten," translating to "All Men's Right." This law means that in public national parks it is everyone's right to take produce off the ground within reason. The Swedes even took foraging to the next level. Where you legally can, even encouraged, to roam the countryside singling out farms with signage of "självplock" or "pick yourself". You essentially go in, pick the produce you want yourself, and pay for it on the way out. In some ways, it puts a new spin on the label "Organic".

Begin with locating the right forest. Here you can find two different forest types: a deciduous forest, or a coniferous forest.

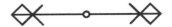

Figure 5 Deciduous Fall Forest, Public Domain

Deciduous forests - see Figure 5 - have a variety of oak, beech, elm, and ash trees. What all of these trees do is shed their leaves as the passage of seasons progresses year by year. Here you don't count time as days or years - you count seasons. But even in deciduous forests, it does not mean that the soil is up to par. Within these shedding forests, the leaves shed brings nutrients to the soil, but is also contingent upon the amount of sunlight being blocked or not blocked. There exist two types of forest-floor soil; Mull and Mor. Perch your nose and take a big whiff if you smell a more sandy smell and hear many leaves rustling about with wind blows, then that means the soil holds little nutrients and is likely acidic. In which case, go mushroom and chanterelle hunting. This is because mushrooms love the Mull, or acidic soil, and uses the thick rug of leaves to keep heat and moisture around them. Mull soils usually thrive in Fall and a bit in the Winter.

Oppositely we have the Spring and Summer seasons. Here, all the leaves should have been decomposed and have delivered their gravy train of nutrients into the ground. Look around if you see few leaves scattered around and you smell that distinct forest floor smell then that means the ground is stock full of nutrients. This soil type is Mor and is where berries and many plants and herbs thrive. In this case, go berry and herb hunting.

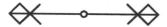

Figure 6 Coniferous Forest, Public Domain

The other type of forest is the coniferous forest – figure 6 above – where trees such as pines and firs are sprouting. What immediately strikes you about these forest covers are two things: the distinct smell of pine and resin, and the dense thick green roof blocking the sun overhead. Here the soil is predominantly Mull, meaning, again, high in acidity and low in nutrients. What you should be on the lookout for are two things; the moisture level of where you are, either from a nearby creek or lake or swamp, and the patches of sunlight created from a windy storm blowing a hole in the tree cover the night prior. If your palette speaks for mushrooms and chanterelles then this forest type is what you want to locate. Especially, go to where creeks, small ponds, or swamps are located. Since the darker green cover, mixed with the acidic Mull soil, and the moisture from the source water is mushrooming paradise for multiplication.

Enough preamble, let's start with what we already have covered in both mor and mull soil; mushrooms, also called chanterelles.

On the mull forest floor, we have a variety of Scandinavian mushrooms littered in the dark damp corners of the mull soil. Just to rapid-fire all the temperate mushrooms you will find, we have the; Common Chanterelle, St. George's Mushroom, Hedgehog Mushroom, Slippery Jack, Bay Bolete, Honey Fungus, Crab Brittlegill, Cep, Yellowfoot, and Wood Blewit. We will hone in on the Common Chanterelle.

The shy charmer who doesn't waste words, who also is the valedictorian of the forest. The Chantelle usually hides underneath pine needles, moss cover, and rotten fallen wood. For years, this mushroom has been the star pupil and greatly sought after for its abundance. But also because it can grow in the winter months. It loves high moisture and usually doesn't grow close to basins of water, so go out and venture for this chanterelle when it has rained for a while. While you cannot mistake the chanterelle from a poisonous variant, there are other offshoots in its stem tree; with a more pale color and the one with a more dark brown color. These can still be picked and eaten but they hold a much more watery taste than our straight-A chanterelle student.

The Common Chanterelle is impressive as a source of Iron and Copper. While also being highly nutritious in Vitamin D and B5. This makes the Common Chanterelle excellent in aiding, for example, brain function. In that Iron fights off risks of dementia and Alzheimer's disease. But the chanterelle also reduces stress, and aids the battle against other mental complications, like anxiety and depression, due to the B5 content. [40]

Now let's move over to the patches of sunlit grounds within the deciduous forest: the jungle of herbs and flowers which are up for grabs.

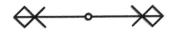

Figure 7 Stinging Nettle, Public Domain

Stinging Nettle, see above figure 7, is quite appropriately named; it stings and burns you when it comes into contact with your skin. Anyone that lives in Northern Europe or America will tell you how much they loathe stinging nettle, mainly due to walking or falling in it many times as children. But hold on, this spiky green plant deserves some recognition. Nettle is truly a blessing and a curse of a plant. Because unbeknownst to many, it actually holds a huge variety of health benefits. Let's have a look.

Nettle is extremely beneficial to females specifically. It is not only beneficial in pregnancy, but also in menopausal and breastfeeding women. It has been shown to aid and regulate female sex hormones such as estrogen and progesterone, but more so estrogen. Nettle is surprisingly rich in iron and can help prevent or even naturally treat anemia. It can also be used as a mild pain reliever as it helps promote muscle healing and is a natural anti-inflammatory. The benefits don't stop here though. As pesky and painful as stinging nettle is, it is actually a healer. Nettle has been shown to reduce the awful debilitating symptoms of rheumatoid arthritis.

To even access the benefits of stinging nettle in the first place, a careful process of handling and harvesting the nettle is needed. Firstly, a thick glove to not get stung, and use a pair of scissors to cut the leaves. You will see small prickly hairs on the leaves, and these are what give stinging nettle its pesky reputation. Once cut, take them home and run them under cold water to rinse off any dirt or bugs. You can boil, cook, or dry the nettle. As long as it is not eaten raw, it is safe to consume. Next, you can boil water and place the leaves in the pot. Boil for around 5 minutes, stirring occasionally.

Nettle is mainly consumed as a tea, but it can also be used as a topping for pasta or other hearty meals. Many have even made their own raw oil from stinging nettle! It can be used as a moisturizer and applied topically on skin and joints. Not many would recognize nettle as a super-herb! But it very much is and on the rise within the Scandinavian fjelle, fjords, woods, and rolling wayside fields.

Scandinavian Nettle and Fish soup is a must-try! It is typically served in Denmark and Sweden, but you may also find this in some parts of Norway.

What you need

Chopped fish of your choice.

1 cup of onion

2 cloves of garlic

2-5 cups (20-50 fl oz) of vegetable or chicken broth

1 tbsp of thyme

1-2 cups of nettle; whole or diced

A pinch of salt and pepper

How to make

On medium heat, add the broth to a large pot, along with the diced fish.

Let it come to a light boil, and simmer for 10 minutes, letting the flavors marinate together.

Add the onion, garlic, thyme, and salt and pepper.

Stir and let cook together for 3 minutes.

Add the nettle, and let cook for an additional 3 minutes.

Turn off the heat and serve! Add toasted bread to the side, or potatoes.

SERVES: 1-2
PREP & COOKING TIME: 15-20 MINUTES

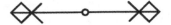

Figure 8 Elderflower and Elderflower juice, Public Domain

Before we go into the wondrous effects of the elderberry and the flower attached Elderflower - get a visual above in figure 8 - a warning if you are going out to forage it in nature. This tree can be confused with a bush that also holds these small white flowers. It so closely resembles that it is called a Dwarf Elder. These Dwarf Elder also have these dark red berries. Do not pick these since these are toxic and can be spotted due to them being a bush. And also, the shape of this berry is different they are more egg-shaped rather than the circular elderberry.

Before we go into the wondrous effects of the elderberry and the flower attached Elderflower - get a visual above in figure 8 - a warning if you are going out to forage it in nature. This tree can be confused with a bush that also holds these small white flowers. It so closely resembles that it is called a Dwarf Elder. These Dwarf Elder also have these dark red berries. Do not pick these since these are toxic and can be spotted due to them being a bush. And also the shape of this berry is different they are more egg-shaped rather than the circular elderberry.

Take a look at just *some* of the benefits of this delicious berry…

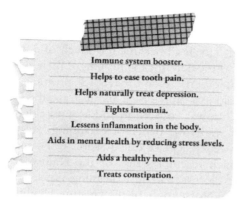

Immune system booster.

Helps to ease tooth pain.

Helps naturally treat depression.

Fights insomnia.

Lessens inflammation in the body.

Aids in mental health by reducing stress levels.

Aids a healthy heart.

Treats constipation.

REPAIRS MUSCLE ACHES.

IT AIDS THE LUNGS & CAN EASE BREATHING PROBLEMS

FIGHTS MIGRAINES

REDUCES FEVER NATURALLY

EASES KIDNEY COMPLICATIONS

REDUCES SEIZURES

REPAIRS SKIN RASHES

TO TOP IT ALL OFF, ELDERBERRY EVEN COMBATS STRONG VIRAL DISEASES SUCH AS AIDS/HIV. [42,43]

What has also been found is that elderberry aids the fight against cancer. This can do wonders for science and your body. [44] Like fighting harmful viruses, it also fights harmful bacteria. [42]

Overall, the elderberry is excellent for protein consumption and aiding your body with essential amino acids, healthy fats, fiber, vitamins, antioxidants, and minerals. Essentially, elderberry's bioactive components aid your body in amazing and restorative ways. Many people use this berry as a way to treat conditions naturally, and many have seen compelling results. [43] This berry may be the healthiest food item in the Scandinavian diet!

Elderberry may be exclusive to Scandinavia, but it was seen being used all the way back to ancient Egypt. Many lifted massive blocks of limestone in the construction of a pyramid. Hard manual labor with the reward of a thrown back and sunburned skin. It all became too much of a nuisance. So the drinking of elderberry was the cure for the healing of their skin. [44] But that doesn't mean that Elderberry didn't have its prominence in the Scandinavian culture. It is said in a Norse Saga about Freja, the Goddess of Fertility and Love, that her hut was covered in and around elderberry trees because of its belief that it wards off dangerous roaming bands of trolls. [45] Likewise, in Southern Sweden, a place called Skåne, or Scania, the word for elderberry is "Hyll" which resembles that of the Danish word for it being "Hyldeblomst" - the 'blomst' part just meaning flower. "Hyll" as a word is said to go back to the Norse myth of the creature Hyldra - a female forest spirit, or dryad, who lived inside of the Elderberry tree protecting it. If a particularly daring Viking would cut down this Elderberry tree for their new Viking longboat or hut, then the Hyll would follow the timber and haunt the owner. The solution that the Norse came up with? Ask permission first, if there was silence then that was construed as permission granted to cut down the tree. [46,47] This mythical link can be connected with the Goddess of Freja as well. It has even been taking a step further of where Freja herself in Sweden and Denmark have been called "Hyl(d)le Mor" meaning 'Elderberry Mother.'

A go-to for kids and adults alike is to drink the elderberry flower as a watery refreshment during the warm summer months. It is deceptively simple but has a sweet floral taste. All you need is 1/4 cup of Elderflower concentrate pressed and squeezed from your freshly foraged Elderflower. Then some ice cubes, the water of your choice, and a lemon slice. Enjoy this beverage in the summer sun.

In Sweden, the berry, the Rowan, has a bit of a fable attached to it - or a Greek fable translated into Swedish to include the Rowanberry. It goes like this, "De är sura, sa räven om rönnbären". It is about a fox trying desperately to reach for a Rowanberry. But the fox cannot, for the life of them, reach it. So they proceed to not admit defeat and say that 'the berry was sour anyways' - walking away perturbed. Funny enough this old legend is where the term "sour grapes" originated. This tale came from Greece, so when it eventually arrived in Sweden, they used the Rowan berries rather than grapes. For one, because few to no grapes could grow in Sweden, and two because the Rowan berries are sour.

The foraging culture both today in 2021 and in the past as pagan Vikings was alive and well. Usually livening up once the weather turns from bone-chilling to just, mildly cold, to go on the hunt for mother nature's free goodies under forest cover.

Here we have children's favorites; blueberries, lingonberries, cloudberries, and bramble berries. We already have covered the first two, so let's delve into the two latter ones. The more arctic grown cloudberry, and the more forested brambleberry.

Cloudberries' etymological name of 'cloud' came from the British merchants in Lancashire speaking about this berry as arriving from the far cold, north, like the sky. The sky holds clouds, and thereby, cloudberry. [48]

Also known as the "gold of the marchland", this berry is as nutritious as they come. Sporting a distinct tart taste, this berry is known for its high content of C vitamin and ellagitannins. [49] Vitamin C we already know all about and the benefits it contains. But ellagitannins definitely are no joke. This ellagic acid has been shown to have anti-inflammatory properties in healing internal wounds. It prevents cancer in your body from forming through antioxidation. Essentially the cloudberry comes striking from the clouds to scourge and removes all the damaged cells in your body caused by oxidation. While it also serves as a prebiotic fiber-strains, which aids your gut health, a commonly neglected area, and immensely boosts your wellbeing and fight against illnesses and diseases in general. And last, but not least, it is cardioprotective, with its polyphenol contents which aid your blood pressure and cholesterol levels to boost your heart health. [50]

In Norway, these cloudberries, or "Mulbær" in Norwegian, are usually turned into a sweet delicious dessert called "Multekrem". It is simple and striking, like the Nordic minimalism. All you need is to stir up some whipped cream, smashed ripe cloudberries, with added sugar. Maybe the Vikings had this simple berry dessert after their "nattmal," or night meal. The food we call dinner today.

The next berry on the picking is **Brambleberry**.

When you go to one of the Scandinavian countries you will experience that foraging is more of a practice than most other countries, namely Sweden due to their abundance of forests. And where there is a market there are businesses. Because in Denmark, for example, you can find apps such as "Byhøst" or "City Harvest" in English, or the newer one; "Vild Mad" or "Wild Food" in English. My particular favorite is the newer Wild Food app, which holds recipes and also holds valuable information on how to smell, feel, and spot high nutrient forest soil from a bad one.

Bramble berries, or in some other parts Blackberries, are wild at night. Not because they grow there but because their stem tree is vast and expansive. Over 100 blackberry variants exist within the Scandinavian forests. Going looking for them you should go to the edges of these forests, in and around farms, and the hedges bordering these farms. They are everywhere and delicious. If of course, they are ripe - otherwise they are very sour.

Humans have been eating Brambleberries since the Neolithic period and for good reason, because they are incredibly dense with health benefits! What I usually answer when asked how healthy Blackberries really are, is that some varieties of Blackberry contain more dietary fiber strains than wholemeal bread. I know we should have cultivated Brambleberries all those years ago when we were changing to farmer-herders.

If you, for example, would ask any botanist today, they would go into a great discussion of the famed Nicholas Culpeper, an English botanist, herbalist, and physician from the mid-1600s. The reason why he became so famous is because of his legacy and Herbal Philosophy. He made common knowledge about healthy herbs and remedies available to the public by translating key medicinal texts from Latin into English. While he also strove to educate the common populace about health and the properties of natural herbs and berries. Just to put it into perspective, the systemization of herbs that he carried out, laid the key groundwork for our modern pharmaceutical system of today. [51]

This guy, Nicholas Culpeper, famously said about the Blackberry that it was a remedy for nearly all ailments and wounds. Let's whizz over a bit to the West from England and venture into Ireland. Blackberry leaves, roots, and the berry themselves were used to treat the common cold, coughs, and the flu, owing to its astringent and antiseptic qualities. Both the benefits from astringent and antiseptics are highly effective in both the look and the health of your skin. It clears out and shrinks pores, tightens the skin, reduces acne, and stops the growth of micro-growths on your skin that can turn into rashes or other signs of damaged skin. [52] Outside of this, Blackberries are full of C vitamin, high in fiber as mentioned, vitamin K, and manganese to aid your bones. [53]

Additionally, some studies have come out that show that Blackberries improve cognitive abilities and prevent memory loss. [54] It can even improve your oral, teeth, and gum health. [55] This tends to be an overall neglected area of the body that not enough people are focusing on. An unhealthy mouth is linked with heart disease, diabetes, lung diseases, and

Alzheimer's. [56] Pretty pivotal.

In Sweden, there is a name of "smultronställe" which refers to that secret, hidden gem of a place that makes you not want to divulge to your neighbor. Loosely this is translated into English as "wild strawberry place". This was because strawberries were so rare to stumble upon and because those delightful reds were so tasty as well.

See, foraging wild herbs, flowers, berries, and other produce is known to hold more vitamins than most food found in supermarkets. In some ways, it is interesting how we as humans developed into modern humans due to the higher availability of food over our technological developments. Peaking, for now, at brick-and-mortar hypermarkets with an added online click promoting same-day delivery. But more times than not, and in higher and higher numbers, we humans are reverting to our roots of picking foraged roots to supplement our consumerism.

It is both enjoying the perks from suburban malls or 1-day shipping, and the health benefits and connection with nature through our gathering without hunting. Mindfully connecting with the 188,000 years we lived as nomadic tribes who hunted and gathered, as opposed to our farmer-herder one for 11,750 years, kicking off the sod in our lungs and in the air through the industrial revolution. One could argue we are in another human epoch right now based on the information and the service industry for if we are being generous, 100 years. The main point, we are hunter-gatherers who gather produce in our carts on a screen or in a hypermarket.

Let's move on to the last part of this chapter and that is tree sap. There are a variety of saps, we are talking all about the deciduous forest sorts of Beech, Oak, Ash, and Birch. Let's highlight one, in particular, taking off: Birch sap, or Birch water.

In the past, when you would go to your local gym and gaze at the overpriced chilled liquids, you would find rows of coconut water. This is for a good reason, coconut and especially its oils are incredibly healthy. Because marketers strive to constantly convince you that you need other, previously unknown stuff, we now have charcoal, maple, and cactus water. But we are talking Scandinavia, so we are highlighting what the next coconut water will turn into and is currently gaining significant strides: Birch water. Even though we have a British company capitalizing on this growing trend, they have admitted that the origins and secrets are from the Scandi-landies. The reason for the Birch tree, as opposed to the other one's, is because Birch is known to absorb copious amounts of water from their surroundings and mix it with the tree's excellent nutrients. Some of which is a high concentration of electrolytes, a collection of minerals found naturally in your blood that aids the overall fluid levels in your whole body. This means that these electrolytes help your body with stabilizing your blood pressure and muscle density. [57]

The Birch tree absorbs in all the moisture in the air, raindrops from the sky, and the water from the ground around it to create the sap. In short, the cleaner and healthier the air and soil is around the Birch tree, the cleaner and healthier the sap is going to be. This is why Birch water as mentioned before contains such a high amount of needed minerals, they are sucked in from the ground and vary depending on how rocky the terrain is around. Outside of that, Birch water has a healthy amount of natural carbohydrates and calories to give you healthy energy, while being high in both vitamin C and B.

Who knew? To home in on one of the restorative minerals, we must discuss one that we have covered before; manganese. See, Birch water of just 300 milliliters - 10.2 ounces, contains 130% of the daily suggested value of manganese that health authorities suggest. What that means is that Birch water is essential both during and after lifting weights and doing cardio. This is because manganese is essential in restoring your body and bone development and maintenance. Also due to the aforementioned blood pressure and muscle density regulation. Side bonuses of Birch water is that it is shown to aid your skin through increased natural production in your body of keratinocytes which directly produces skin cells. Likewise, Birch water also has a positive effect on your hair through the aid of your natural production of collagen and iron absorption in your body. [58]

When you know all these benefits of this super-water you begin to understand the folklore and the past around this majestic slender peeling white tree.

Thor, the most well-known Norse God thanks to Stan Lee, originally was associated with the Birch tree - whereas Thor was, outside of thunder and lightning, believed to be the protector of humankind and strength in general. Makes sense for the pumping iron juice mentioned earlier. The sap in the past was made into the Viking drink of choice; mead, which you read all about in the "Mulled Wine and Mead" chapter. Likewise, glue was also made from Birch to produce arrowhead and flint axes. While the Birch tree bark was also used to build roofs and even commonly used to smoke meat and fish. [59] If you want to learn about the art of smoked poultry, whizz down to the "Smokin' Hot" chapter.

5

SMOKIN' HOT

Figure 9 My brother and I on the smoking island of Bornholm, a Danish Island

Naturally, it changes from Scandi to Scandi, but it is rare that I have stumbled upon a fellow Scandi and heard that they did not like the taste of smoked food. As you will soon learn, smoking was used by everyone. But the Nordic lands had a profundity for it.

When trotting through the dotted fishing hamlets on the coastline of Bornholm. For a visual of young adult me, and young adult my brother, see figure 9. You are struck by the windy idyllic charm of the old 1700s cottages dictated by the rocky terrain of where they are located. But throughout your sightseeing and the friendly smiles from the locals, you will see these jutting, white chimneys everywhere. And you can't help but notice a distinct smokey smell when close to them. These are smokers where usually fish, and namely herring, are being smoked, preserving the traditional ways of both hot and cold smoking. Although today most of these are either owned by or linked to a seafood restaurant to get the famed gastronomical experience of smoked herring. Welcome to the smoked world of Scandinavia. In this chapter, we cannot make you smell this distinct smell, so a wordy experience has to suffice...

History of smoked food.

It didn't take long before the human race realized that meat from animals needed to be preserved - moldy, spoiled meat is not the greatest for both the taste buds and the gut health. We can thank the OG of ancestors for smoking techniques, as they were the first to implement them... some 2 million years ago. [60–62]

People soon learned that smoking the meat would keep the meat fresh and edible for much longer. Finally, taking a day off from hunting was a possibility in conjunction with the breaded revolution - written about later in this book. Not long after, they added salt and drying techniques and found that the meat would keep for even longer. But there was one problem. Smoking took time, and you could not have your smoked meat to-go, as it could sometimes take days of exposing the meat to smoke. Which posed a problem as roaming tribal hunter-gatherer people, constantly moving where conditions were best.

But smoking persisted and was eventually adopted into all kinds of cultures all over the world, the reasoning anthropologists and archeologists speculate was so that early establishments and the tribes could make trade a possibility between each other. As time went on and we entered into the modern age, our need for smoking diminished thanks to refrigerators and freezers. So smoking food is today now done purely for the taste. Likely due to hundreds of thousands of years of smoking, our biology and reward-centers in our brain was hardwired to say, "this smoked taste is rather enjoyable".

The Scandinavian countries mirrored this in the same way as the act of smoking. Although the freezing parts of Scandinavia, such as the arctic circle, rarely needed smoking. This was because these tribes preserved meat in animal skin beneath the frozen sea and lakes. The precursor to the fridge-freeze. The other parts of Scandinavia, namely the warmer and more temperate areas of Norway and Sweden, could not employ both a smoked technique and salting, due to that salt was rare. This resulted in being smoked and not salted, and they began to ferment and is why we have the Swedish, fermented fish "Surströmming". [63] If you don't know what this is, then simply look up people who have just sniffed "Surströmming". Immense fun can be had.

See the reason why these northern fish started to ferment, or in plain Anglo-Saxon lingo; rot, was because the smoking techniques back then were known as 'cold smoking'. Essentially, placing meat or fish or anything else they fancied in an air-sealed room to fill this moderately warm room with A LOT of smoke. How this could be achieved was by producing the smoke in a separate heat-insulated chamber or room. While then have the smoke directed to another moderately warm room. This was how the Scandinavian smoked their food for years and years. [63]

Today many artisans have adopted the art of smoking, partially for the flavor and the other as a hobby. You can see later on in this book the modern household method of smoking if you want to venture into the art of smoking.

The benefits and science behind smoked food.

So how does it happen? Well for starters, there are various methods on how you can smoke meat. You can do it hot, cold, or even warm. There's also liquid and smoke roasting. Whatever method you decide on, all smoking methods have the same basic principles. Smoke seeps into the meat, and it is done slowly. The smoke then breaks down collagen, making the meat a lot more tender, rich with flavor, and preserves the meat for a lot longer.

The only time when smoking is considered constructive is when it is done to meat. As we all know, smoking kills, and lucky for us it hunts down all kinds of bacteria found on meat. It stops fat from going rotten and prevents mold from forming. It also makes it inhospitable so new bacteria cannot move in when the old ones die. This is because smoking meats suck all of the moisture out. [64]

The immense flavor one can get from smoking meat is on another level. This flavor goes hand in hand with the breaking down of the collagen making the meat more tender. The smoking also then melts the fat, fusing it with the meat for your pallet to having an explosion of fusion flavor when enjoying it. We humans enjoy a sense of smokiness once in a while. This could be thanks to great memories we had around bonfires, or even due to the ancestral memories in the limbic system of our brain, dating back to when our caveman ancestor's serotonin levels shot up when they discovered the magic of fire. The bottom line, anything with a smoky tang to it. Whether it be sitting around a bonfire, eating smoked food, or enjoying the smoky taste of a glass of Scotch whiskey... the smoky flavor has been wired into our brains to be something pleasurable. [64]

Let us not forget the modern benefit of vacuum-packed smoked meat. If you buy it one day, you'll still have a few weeks to eat it without having to freeze it.

The Nordic method.

As mentioned above, smoking food was a way of preserving meat. A tactic discovered by our Paleolithic ancestors. They smoked the area where the meat was kept to keep pests and scavengers at bay and accidentally figuring out that it is a great way to preserve meat and give it that extra flavor. [60]

How the Scandinavians smoked their food and what they used.
There were various methods to smoking food in the Viking times, but the most preferred method was smokehouses. Other methods were more designed for cooking food through smoking methods, such as the "Plankefisk" (plank fish), which was made by nailing a fish to a wooden board just above an open fire. [65]

The smokehouses used for preservation were miniature wooden cabins built a few feet above the ground, sort of like a small treehouse. They were built this way to keep animals away and stop them from eating their stockpiled meat. [66]

The modern vs. ancient methods.

As I had mentioned above, smoking in the olden days was done using smokehouses being built above ground to keep wild animals at bay. Luckily in modern times, keeping wild animals away from meat is a little easier than before.

Smokehouses today are much cleaner and visually aesthetic. Not to mention that every product produced today must go through rigorous health and safety standards to make sure everything is up to standard. Who knows what bacteria and parasites the old smokehouses opened their doors to. Smokehouses are also passed through very strict quality testing so you can sleep well at night knowing the quality of your smokehouse is up to code.

We have quite a bit more control over modern-day smokehouses as we can accurately control the temperature and the consistency of the smoke. Smoking can even be done from a portable barbeque stand, depending on which one you decide to invest in.

Smokehouses in this day and age can also be built for smaller personal use, or even on a bigger industrial scale.

Figure 10 Propane smoker by Dennis Brown, Wikimedia Commons [67]

A traditional Norwegian smoked dish is smoked salmon. This can easily be achieved at home with wood chips and a charcoal or gas grill if you do not have a smoker, like the one above on figure 10.

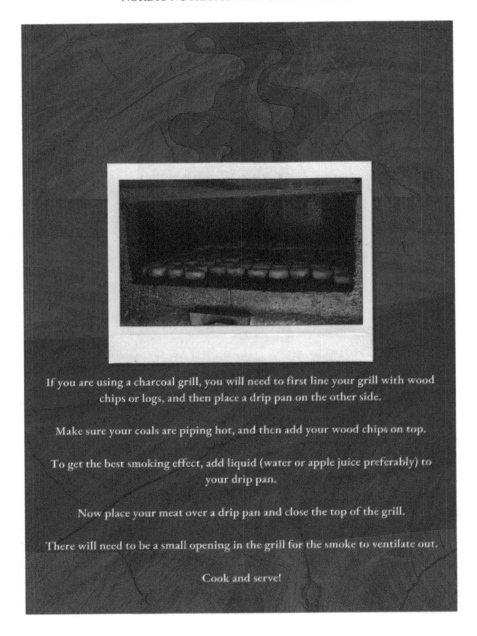

If you are using a charcoal grill, you will need to first line your grill with wood chips or logs, and then place a drip pan on the other side.

Make sure your coals are piping hot, and then add your wood chips on top.

To get the best smoking effect, add liquid (water or apple juice preferably) to your drip pan.

Now place your meat over a drip pan and close the top of the grill.

There will need to be a small opening in the grill for the smoke to ventilate out.

Cook and serve!

Air ventilation is key for the smoked meat to be a success. If there is no ventilation, then the smoke will eventually burn the meat due to the high temperature, leaving a charred burned taste, rather than a smoky delicious taste. What you want is for the meat to be juicy and tender. A mix of air and smoke will create the perfect balance in your meat.

Wood is also an essential key in creating perfectly smoked meat at home. You can use different types of wood, based on which type of meat you are cooking. The Vikings likely didn't have this luxury of different types of wood, but we do now! You can chop your own, or buy them pre-cut. Let's take a look at each wood type you can use at home...

Wood chips.

Wood chips are probably the most common type used with at-home smoking. With this wood type, it is perfect for meat that will be smoked for 2-4 hours. The general rule is that, if the wood pieces are thin, they will not last long. For thick meat that requires all-day smoking, you will need to use something a bit thicker. To prevent the wood from burning, you can soak it in water beforehand as this is quite effective. [68]

Wood chunks.

Thick meat that will be smoked all day, will cook best on thicker wood chunks. These could be moderate-sized logs that you have cut yourself or have bought pre-cut. This is for those that really want to embrace their Nordic ancestors! As the chunks are thicker and larger, they will burn for longer and will create even more smoke. Again, feel free to soak the logs in water before cooking. If you are planning on smoking your meat for more than a couple of hours, you must change out your wood and charcoal every couple of hours to prevent them from burning to a crisp. [68]

Wood pellets or pieces.

This is for those that only want a slight smokiness flavor for their food. The wood pellets burn quickly and are designed for pellet smokers. [68] So you essentially have 3 sizes and choices; small, medium, and large, all designed to fit your smoking needs.

The temperature while smoking does not have to be as hot as a typical grill. Smoking food requires patience, which means low/medium heat over a long time. Try to aim for 200-250 degrees (90-120 Celsius). And flipping your meat is actually not necessary, because smoking will cook your meat thoroughly and evenly. But if you're unsure, you can keep a meat thermometer handy. And feel free to season your meat to your liking before placing it in your grill, and make sure the meat is room temperature, not cold or frozen. You can smoke other food such as seafood, veggies, or cheese as well. Get creative with it!

6

THAT SWEET TOOTH

The ancient Scandinavians were more than just the brutes you all know and love. A lot of them, like you and me, had a sweet tooth. See with food not being able to be kept as long as it can in the modern days, the Nordic folk was very creative with all the ingredients they could find, hunt, and gather. So, when it came time for dessert, they mainly used the following ingredients and only splotched when it was strictly necessary. [69]

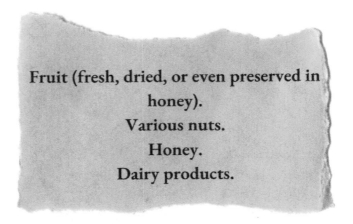

Fruit (fresh, dried, or even preserved in honey).
Various nuts.
Honey.
Dairy products.

Why were Scandinavians so great at baking?

Possibly the most important aspect and the biggest secret as to why the Scandinavian folk was able to produce such amazing baked goods, was due to their resourceful nature. Never did they overload their sweet stuff with an abnormal amount of sugar. Instead, they practiced and practiced until they got the right amount of the above ingredients to make an explosion of flavor in your mouth. [70]

Figure 11 Cinnamon Roll, Kanelbulle, Public Domain

One such example is the creation of the cinnamon roll, see figure 11 above. Which in ancient times was a lot less sticky and had a lot less sugar in the simpler times. In general, cinnamon was mostly used in ancient times as a medicinal herb and as a strong fragrant. For example, archeologists have found cinnamon residue on the Egyptian mummies, imported from China. Clearly to shield the stomach-churning odor of a chemically preserved Egyptian pharaoh or upper-crust person. [71]

The cinnamon spice was first realized by the Roman empire. Or rather the Roman spice merchants, traveling up and down the Silk road, and on the scurvy-filled high seas to make a buck from selling Sri Lankan and Indian Cassia Cinnamon, as it is known. [71] It was, therefore, a highly expensive spice and only the upper crusts of Scandinavia could afford to spice their food and desserts up with it. So, as the spice became more readily available, so too was the cinnamon roll more readily available. Conceived in Sweden under the name "kanelbulle". Swedish marketers even wanted to take it up a notch and introduced through marketing in 1999 that October 4th was known as 'kanelsbulle dag' or cinnamon roll day. Partially to increase sales in Sweden of these rolls. But to also promote Swedish pastries abroad, the cinnamon roll included - making the roll synonymous to Sweden. As the creator, Kaeth Gardestedt, said when asked about this day - just, you know in Swedish, "A thought with Cinnamon Roll Day was that it would be a day of thoughtfulness." [72]

Health benefits of cinnamon

Actually, Cassia cinnamon, like many other spices and herbs, is incredibly healthy for you. But in a full-blown contest of 26 spices ranking them and tracking all the benefits, cinnamon came out as the clear champion! Even beating that of garlic and turmeric, which are known as superfoods. [73] Just to put cinnamon into perspective, and why it should be on your top supplements list, the strength of cinnamon in preserving naturally organic and bio-cultural material means that it can be used as a natural food preservative! [74]

To mention the main properties, it is amazing for your digestive and gut health. Cinnamon, in general, helps the natural processes and gastric juices to be secreted in your stomach. Which have been linked with helping with… [71,75–77]

Acid reflux.
Stomach ulcers.
Excessive gas.
Digestion of food.
Vomiting in general.

Cinnamon has one of the highest concentrations of effective blood cleaners and potent polyphenol antioxidants, which we will circle back to time and time again for your health. [78–80]

Essentially what that means is that it protects your cells' natural defense against cellular damage and aids your own natural cleaning of inert or dead cells in your bloodstream which increases as we age. In other words, cinnamon is a natural anti-age remedy and maximizes your potential healthy lifespan.

This wonder spice helps your own natural hormones that work to reduce your insulin resistance, helping you prevent type-2 diabetes, which is a rampant illness on the rise. [81,82]

Cinnamon is a natural antibacterial and has even been shown to reduce the risk of cancer in mice. [83] Cinnamon can also aid respiratory complications and diseases caused by fungal growths, and cinnamon oil extract is known to prevent you from getting these nasty bacterial surprises. [84,85] Incredible enough, cinnamon has even shown to fight against the incurable viral disease HIV! [86]

How to make Swedish traditional cinnamon rolls: "Kanelsbulle"

Serves: 2-3
Prep Time: 40 Minutes – 1 Hour
Cooking Time: 30 Minutes

Here is what you will need to make the dough…

- 2 cups (450 grams) of wheat, or all-purpose, flour.
- 1/3 - 80 grams of fine sugar.
- 1 and ½ teaspoon (7 grams) of yeast.
- 1/2 tablespoon (5 grams) of fresh cardamom.
- 1/2 teaspoon (3 grams) of salt.
- 1 cup (250 grams) of chilled whole milk.
- 1 egg whisked in a bowl.
- 1/2 cup (100 grams) of chilled butter cut from a knife, preferably into small cubes for the best result.

And here is how to go about it with the dough…

1. Mix together the flour, sugar, yeast, and cardamom in a bowl and begin to stir thoroughly. Once mixed, add the salt and stir some more.

2. Once done, add the chilled whole milk and your whisked egg in a pan or pot to gently heat it up. Do not let it boil, only get it to lukewarm

heat. Then add your flour mix from step one and it will create a dough.

3. If you have a mixing machine then this will be much easier, otherwise, you will have to have a ripped forearm. Now place the dough in a mixer, stirring gently, and add the cubed butter one by one. The general rule is to stir for about 3 minutes for each cube thrown in there.

4. Once you have added all your butter cubes, feel your dough. If it is too sticky then add, moderately, more flour, until your dough has a somewhat sticky substance - but not too much. You want to aim for slightly sticky to the touch.

5. Then move the dough over to a bowl with a bit of oil on its side. Cover your bowl and place it in a lukewarm and dry place for it to double in size. This takes, depending on conditions, about an hour.

And here is how to go about it with the cinnamon filling and the rolling...

What you will need first is...

- 1/3 cup (80 grams) of soft butter.
- 1 teaspoon of wheat, or general flour.
- 1 tablespoon of fresh cinnamon.
- 1 teaspoon of vanilla sugar.
- 1/5 cup (40 grams) of normal sugar.

Okay, here is how to go about this...

1. Begin to preheat your oven to about 450 Fahrenheit or 225 Celsius.

2. Once your dough has finished doubling in size, knead it out on a lightly floured counter. What you want to aim for in the roll-out is a rectangle of about 20 x 16 inches, or 50 x 40 centimeters.

3. Now take out a bowl and mix the butter, flour, cinnamon, and sugars. Once mixed, spread it over your rectangle dough.

4. Begin from the side and gently roll your cinnamon topped rectangle dough to create a 20 inch or 50 centimeters long sausage. Then take a sharp knife and begin to cut even pieces, to resemble a roll. Place your rolls on to a prepared baking tray, place something over them - I recommend a cloth - and place them in a lukewarm, dry place, to double in size; 60 minutes usually does the trick.

5. Place the buns in the oven for 25 minutes, and check regularly on the buns. You want a light golden-brown coloration, not a dark burned one.

While your rolls are baking you can take your time to prepare the icing and the finishing touches…

What you will need is…

- 1 egg.
- 1 teaspoon of any kind of milk.
- 1/4 cup of chilled water.
- 1/4 teaspoon of vanilla extract or paste.
- 1/5 cups or 45 grams of sugar.
- 2 teaspoons of pearl sugar.

Now, how to prepare…

1. Begin with whisking your egg and milk together. 15 minutes before your rolls are done, take out your rolls briefly, when they have hardened a bit, and paint your rolls with your egg and milk mix. Then put them back in and let them finish baking for about 10 minutes. Your buns should turn golden brown.

2. While your last stretch of baking is happening, heat up your water, sugar, and vanilla paste in a pot until it boils. But always stir when your mix is hitting the boiling point. What you want is for all the sugar to have completely dissolved in your pot-mix.

3. Take out your finished rolls, glaze them with the mix you made in step 2, and sprinkle some pearl sugar on top as well. Set them to cool off with something over it, to not become dry and stale. After a few

minutes when going from piping hot to lukewarm, enjoy both your rolls and the praises from your family, friends, colleagues, or your neighborhood!

The history and culture of the cheese Danish and the Easter fastening bun

The other such famous invention of a Scandinavian popular pastry is the spandauer, or weinerbrød, or fastelavnsbolle, or a Danish, or cheese Danish in America. To get down this rabbit hole of this pastry is to go down in an utter state of confusion. Let's get the easy one out of the way. The reason why in the United States that it is called a cheese Danish is because the recipe was brought over from Danish immigrants going to the New World. Okay, that was the easy one - hold on tight, because this is going to get complicated, real fast.

See outright befuddlement begins when we trace back the Danish names of this fluffy pastry. Of which in Denmark, we have three different names for the same pastry, I know, of: "spandauer", "weinerbrød", and "fastelavnsbolle". The first two are said interchangeably, where the latter one is connected to the Easter holiday in Denmark. To add to the confusion, both the names "weinerbrød" and "spandauer" have a German linguistic flair to them.

Let's begin with "spandauer". This one is named after the German suburban city of Berlin, Spandau. Or rather, the German prison complex. Why is this? Because this famous Spandau prison, with the same name as the city, has four towers around its complex - like most prisons, but I digress. The thought was invented because the pastry dough is trapped between four towers like the Spandau prison. So the name "spandauer" came about. [87]

This brings us to the other name, "weinerbrød". See actual invention of the cheese Danish was not made in Denmark. The pastry itself is traced back to Vienna, Austria. Vienna in Danish is "Wien" and is where the name "weinerbrød" comes from. In a rough translation to English, it would be "Viennese Bread".

Here is the historical background: All Danish bakers in 1850 decided to carry out a nationwide strike, not showing up for work and no bread being baked. The owners of these bakeries needed the flow of bread to be made for the hungry Danish populace. So rather than wait until the strike was over and the bakers got what they demanded, they hired abroad and got, among others, Austrian bakers into Denmark to bake. Through this hiring, the Austrian bakers brought with them the recipe for the spandauer, or weinerbrød, or fastelavnsbolle, or cheese Danish, and began to introduce this delightful puffy pastry to the Danes. Everyone knew it came from Vienna, so the generalized name became "weinerbrød", where it seems that within the baking profession "spandauer" is the name. Although, the actual pastry dough got innovated on and became a Danish creation to give it that fluffy texture. [88]

What gets muddled is that the pastry became so widespread in the world from Denmark that even in Vienna, the birthplace of the sweet itself it is known as "Dänischer Plunder, or Kopenhagener Plunder".

Figure 22 Danish Easter holiday pastry, Wikimedia Commons [89]

When the Easter holiday in Scandinavia rolls over the rolling hills and mountains and forests, you will frequently hear a soft knock on your door. You walk over to your door and immediately you are met with between 2 to 4 kids, all dressed in mainstream pop-culture getups. Or the classics of princess or Zorro or Superman. Upon seeing the cosplay mini's, you hear their high-pitched voices sing, "Boller op, boller ned - boller i min mave! Hvis jeg ikke boller får, så laver jeg ballade!"

Translated to: 'Buns up, buns down - buns in my tummy! If I don't get my buns, then rumpus will be made!' A smile creeps over your face and you hand out candy to the kids, they politely say thanks and move on to the next house. In some ways, this custom is the Scandinavian version and the non-spooky version of Halloween. Oh and these greatly sought-after buns are the traditional cheese Danish; although back then they were more like normal wheat buns. See figure 12 above. Because wheat buns far back in the day were considered a luxury and something uniquely special.

The last, and more topical Easter holiday name of "fastelavnsbolle", roughly translates to 'the fasting bun'. Historically in Denmark, linked with a Catholic tradition, was that you needed to eat as much as you could before you would fast for 40 days. It is even said that the Swedish king Adolf Frederik in 1771 passed from eating one too many of these fastening buns. Nicknamed "the king who ate himself to death", this real-life fairy tale almost has a gluttonous symbolism behind it. Thinking back to the classics of Brother Grimm or H.C. Andersen.

Speaking of Sweden, "in det avlånga landet", or oblong nation, the fastening bun equivalent is called semla. Or if being a bit playful; fettisdagbulle, literally meaning 'fat Tuesday roll'. Whereas in Norway, it echoes that of Denmark, more in the naming scheme of 'fastelavnsbolle' as well. Although, Norway and Sweden's actual pastry mirrors that of each other. With a cut-off top, more traditional wheat dough, sweetened almond paste, and whip cream on top. But we will get to the recipe.

Today very few Scandinavian folks, if any at all, fast during this Easter tradition. As mentioned, in the past, the fasting bun was actually not the same as the cheese Danish. There were similarities, but not the same - see the picture above in figure 12. The traditional fastening bun is closed off and contains fillings inside with icing on top. The cheese Danish has more of a wall around a crater filled with cream cheese and decorated with all sorts of things; icing crunched nuts, whatever the heart desires. The fastening bun has just become synonymous with this Easter holiday, as to be considered the same pastry by many Danes.

The oldest believed fastening bun to have been found was on a church mural dating back to the year 1250. But it is believed that the actual bun was just a wheat bun, very different from the pastry sweet we know today. But it is said that the fastening bun actually originates from Germany since the church chalk mural is disputed as something else. The closed of fastening bun has therefore been tracked to the German bun called "heisswecke", meaning 'warm opening'. This opening got warm at the beginning of the 1600s in Northern Germany and is said to have moved its way further north to Denmark later on. [90,91] Over time, new variants of the fastening bun, even the different Scandinavian countries mix and match their special breed of pastry bun. In Sweden, the fastening bun sports whip cream and is sometimes sliced in the middle to resemble a sandwich.

After going through this linguistic, although delicious, rabbit hole, I should be handed an honorable linguist doctorate...

Figure 33 Easter fastening pastry Public Domain

How to make the cheese Danish and the fastening bun

The oldest discoverable recipe of the Danish fastening bun is called "Madam Mangors" and dates back to 1857, see figure 13 above, to get a visual...

What you need

3 eggs.

2 ounces (60 grams) of sugar.

6.7 ounces (190 grams) of butter.

1.7 ounces (50 grams) of yeast.

17.5 - 0.5 liter of lukewarm sweetened milk.

2.2 pounds (1 kilogram) of wheat flour.

0.5 pounds (250 grams) of organic raisins.

1.7 ounces (50 grams) of finely chopped orange peel.

Half a teaspoon of both cinnamon and cardamom.

How to make

Whisk all the eggs together with the sugar, to create a sugary egg mass.

Melt the butter in a pot, and pour the melted butter into the sugary mass.

In the same pot, place the yeast and sweetened milk to dissolve in the yeast in the milk while lightly stirring. When done, pour the yeasted milk into the sugary egg and butter mass.

SERVES: 2-3
PREP/COOKING TIME: 1 HOUR

Now slowly and in increments pour the wheat flour into the mass while stirring. Your goal is to hit a nice moist baking dough.

Place the dough in a lukewarm place with a cloth over it and wait until it has grown to double its size.

Take the dough and massage the raisins, orange peel, cinnamon, and cardamom into the dough.

When the filling is nicely spread out and spread out throughout the dough, take off small hand-palm-sized chunks of the dough and begin to roll them in your hand to make round buns. When done, place the unbaked buns in the same lukewarm place with a cloth over it to let them bloom in size once more.

After the buns are finished growing, paint them with egg yolk, and sprinkle some sugar on top as well. After fashioning the buns, bake them at 390 Fahrenheit or 200 degrees Celsius until the buns are nice and golden brown.

SERVES: 2-3
PREP/COOKING TIME: 1 HOUR

Side tip, the fashioning of the sugar was just the old choice, you can deep-dive into any toppings that suit your fancy. It can be from crushed almonds to icing, to jams.

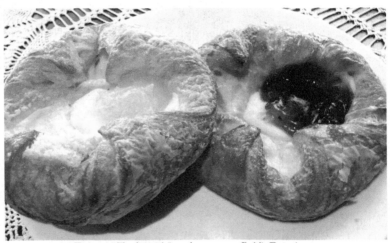

Figure 44 Traditional Spandauer pastry, Public Domain

Next up is the recipe for the spandauer, see figure 14 above for a mouth-watering visual reference.

Here you will need...

Quick side note before we go into the recipe itself.

Make sure you have all of the ingredients prepared before you go into baking this famous, delicious pastry. Likewise, you will have to make some choices before you begin to make the spandauer dough. Decide on what kind of filling in the middle you would want, is it jam, cream cheese, or maybe something else? Have all of the prepared ingredients ready. Put the measured flour in the freezer, the egg yolk in the fridge, and so on. It is a bit complicated and consists of two parts, but you will figure out that it is fully worth it.

Serves: 2-4
Prep Time: 1 hour 10 minutes
Cooking Time: 30 minutes

For the dough, you will need...

- 1/8 cups - 40 grams of yeast.
- 3/4 cups - 2 deciliters of water.
- 3/4 cups - 2 deciliters of egg yolk.
- 1/3 - 75 grams of sugar.
- 1/8 cup - 15 grams of salt.
- 2.5 cups - 625 grams of wheat flour.

Note to always put the water, egg yolk, and flour in for cooling in the fridge the day before baking.

For the kneading, you will need...

- 2.5 cups - 625 grams of butter.
- Plus a little extra wheat flour to use as a powdery bed for the finished, ready to be kneaded dough.

For the filling, icing, and the finishing touch you will need...

- 3/4 cup - 150 grams of marzipan.
- 1/2 cup - 100 grams of sugar.
- 1/2 cup - 100 grams of butter.
- 1 egg 5. 1 pinch of salt.
- 1 tablespoon of water.
- 1/3 cup - 75 grams of hazelnut flakes.
- 3/4 cup - 200 grams of powdered sugar.
- 1 and 2/3 cups - 5 deciliters of milk.

Now, how you would go about making this pastry is a bit complicated, or the pastry dough itself is a bit complicated. But just follow along, and take it slow...

1. (This pastry will go so much smoother if you have a mixer or blender.) First, smolder the yeast into a bowl. Now add the cold eggs,

sugar, salt, and the freezer cold flour.

2. Begin to stir but only so it is partially mixed together, don't over stir. And then place the clump of dough on a bed of wheat flour.

3. Now smear a bit of butter on your table - try not to break up the butter, but have it be a solid square - with a bit of wheat flour so the butter doesn't stick too much on your table.

4. Take your butter square and gently place it on top, like a hat, on the clump of dough. Once done, begin to gently hit the butter into the dough.

5. When the butter is thoroughly attached to the dough, begin to fold the dough in on itself. What you want is for the dough to completely encompass the butter.

6. Begin now to hit the dough so the butter very lightly is visible on the side. Drizzle plenty of wheat flour, both on top of the dough and under, and begin to knead the dough flat into a square.

7. As a square, remove all excess flour and fold the four corners in so all four corners meet and tough each other in the middle. The end result should look like a smaller square now that has been tilted 45-degrees. Knead it out flat and place it in the fridge for about 15 minutes.

8. Take your, now cold, square out of the fridge and knead it out, with a bit of flour to a rectangle elongated square. Because now you have to fold this together into a perfect square. Take a knife and mark lines on the elongated square into three parts. Take one of the sides - 1/3 of the square - from your line and fold it in to meet the other line, and do the same for the other side - the other 1/3. What you want is three layers of dough on top of each other still connected. Place it back into the fridge for about 15-minutes.

9. Do it once again, so you now have many layers of dough folded in on each other making one perfect square. This is what creates the fluffy, moist texture of the pastry. Note that all the ingredients and dough that you work with have to be cold at all times.

Now to make the cream cheese or filling, what gives the pastry its sweet surprise...

1. Mix together sugar, raw vanilla corn, and starch in a bowl. Now add 1/3 cup or 1 deciliter of milk to then whisk it thoroughly together in the bowl. And at the end, add the egg yolk.

2. Take the remainder of your milk and place it in a pot to boil it with the emptied, raw vanilla stick.

3. When it boils add the mix you made in step 1 to the pot and whisk thoroughly until you see the substance turn into a thick cream.

4. Take the pot off the heat and pour the boiling hot cream into a cold canister, place a lid over the canister and place the canister to be cooled down in the fridge. You can use the cream later that same day or the day after.

The other part of the filling…

1. Take the marzipan and sugar, and put it in a large bowl. Begin to knead them together to one mass, while you bit by bit add butter to the mix. What you want is to create one consistent substance.

Okay, pat yourself on the back, because you are done with the prepping phase. Now it is time to assemble.

1. Take your pastry dough from the fridge and knead it out so it is about 4 millimeters or .1 inch in thickness.

2. Take a knife and begin now to cut squares out from the kneaded dough, so they resemble the size of about 4x4 inches or 10x10 centimeters.

3. Put the marzipan filling in a disposable syringe bag, and cut a hole in it so you have mindfully squeezed it out in the middle, which you should do now.

4. Then fold the four squared corners in to meet in the middle, as you do in an old letter with the opening facing up, and place them a decent ways apart from each other on your baking pan.

The finishing touch is to paint your unbaked pastries...

1. Whisk together eggs, with salt, and water to make one single substance.

2. Take a paintbrush and paint evenly every unbaked pastry with your egg-salt-water paint.

3. Once done press a small crater in the middle of each pastry meant to be filled with your vanilla cream from the fridge.

4. Fill up your crater with the vanilla cream from a disposable syringe bag, and fashion the pastries with some almond flakes.

5. Place all of your cheese Danish pastries in a lukewarm place for about 1-hour to grow, and then place them in a preheated oven at 375 Fahrenheit or 190 Celsius, for about 20 minutes. Check occasionally on your work and see if your pastry buns are turning golden brown on top and hard and crusty on the bottom.

6. Once they are golden, take them out and place them on your kitchen counter to cool off.

While waiting for delicious cheese Danish pastries to cool off, so you can surprise your family, or dinner guests, or colleagues, you can make some icing for them. Just mix powdered sugar and a bit of water, alternatively slowly add water while you whisk it together in a pot being heated up. Once the icing looks, well, like icing, smear it on your pastries with a knife and bask in your traditional cheese Danish, "spandauer," "wienerbrød," "fastelavnsboller," or "semla" sweet pastry bun. Enjoy!

Red porridge with cream

Traditionally, Dane's have immense fun listening to the pronunciation attempts of this traditional dessert "rødgrød med fløde", or red porridge with cream. In fact, this custom of national identity, based on a phrase or a word in a particular language, is within linguistic circles known as a shibboleth. These have been used commonly through wartime to quickly identify friend or foe. But it can today in perpetual peacetime be used within sub-groups of people, like the sub-gaming culture of Fortnite has its own vocabulary, likewise within rock and roll, and so on. Nevertheless, this liquid dish is deceptively simple, like many other variants where minimalism found its birthplace. But is refreshing and sweet nonetheless. Red porridge with cream is considered to be the national dessert and would no doubt be on a test if applying for a citizen Visa in Denmark. It is also not a porridge but never mind the linguistics.

Serves: 1-2
Prep Time: 10 Minutes
Cooking Time: 5 Minutes

All you need is 14 ounces (400 grams) of strawberry, and 10.5 ounces (300 grams) of rhubarb, 3.5 ounces (100 grams) of sugar, 2 spoonful's of starch, and 4 spoons of water. At last, either as much or as little cream at whatever density of fat you prefer or your health dictates.

This is how you prepare...

1. You rinse both the strawberry and the rhubarb under cold running water. Then remove any bits you don't want to smash together; like leaves and ends.

2. Place both the strawberries and the rhubarb in a pot, with the sugar. Then let it simmer in the pot. Check occasionally on the substance, what you want is not a fully liquid-y substance but of slightly squashed.

3. Take your water and your corn starch, and stir the two into a small bowl. Once done, pour the water-starch into the pot and stir in the pot to mix it together.

4. Have it simmer for about one minute, then take it off the heat to slowly cool off. Done!

You can both eat it hot or cold, that is up to you while experimenting with different fashions such as orange slices. Enjoy!

Likewise, we have the other simplistic dessert or snack or breakfast: koldskål, or translated to "cold bowl". But like it is the case with the above 'red porridge with cream' it is actually not a porridge and more a soup. Koldskål is the same; it is a cold fresh soup. Although, before we go into this cold delight, let's see where it started.

Because contrary to popular belief for many Danes, koldskål started out being made from either fruit juice, wine, or even beer. But, and seemingly unrelated, a change in milk products in Denmark occurred in the 1920s from which buttermilk was seen as fodder for pigs. Businesses, at this time, wanted snew variants of milk that could be sold to the Danish public so they started to advertise this buttermilk as human food rather than feed for pigs. In tandem, new recipes and innovations of recipes began to pop up as well. And here is where the new variant of "koldskål" came to be, from acidic milk rather than fruit or grape juice, or beer. [92]

Additionally, koldskål has a best friend that always goes with the dessert bowl; kammerjunker, or translated 'chamberlains'. These are small, round cookies as dry as cracker-treats with a vanilla taste that kids crumble into their koldskål and adults just dump in there. But now you may feel and think "wait, you are just going to skirt over this abundantly strange name of "chamberlains"? Why? Was this cold bowl the dessert dish only for the nobility?" Well, here it is.

First of all, chamberlains, yes, were nobility - but they were the lowest rank within the aristocracy in Denmark. They usually served either the higher-ranking servants or the outright ladies and lords of the house. But this title became more a generic title, akin to what "Sir" or "Ma'am" is in English - a sign of respect. I will say though, if you are ever vacationing in Denmark, don't call people "kammerjunkere". It is not a slur, but Danes will think it charming because it is a person who thinks they have found a respectful generic term for people. The term "kammerjunk" for someone hasn't been used since the 1940s and even back then it was rare. Overall, and we don't know why. But it is speculated that the reason why these sweet cracker-cookies are called 'chamberlains' was that it was a normal dish that they ate while on their lunch breaks. [93]

Figure 55 Koldskål by (c) Skandi Baking [94]

How "koldskål" – see figure 15 from Nordic Food Living [95] - is made is even simpler than "rød grød med fløde", or the red porridge with cream - figure 15 above for a visual. You will need 2 cups of buttermilk, 1 cup of either non-flavored yogurt or skyr, and 3 spoons of sugar.

Then you just whisk all the ingredients together and serve it with some chamberlains. If you cannot find these, then strawberries, a slice of lemon, and rhubarb also go well with the dish.

Health benefits and science behind Scandinavian sweets

It is no shocker that the fruit section of the Viking sweet diet was so healthy and beneficial for you. To prove the point even further, we'll list the health benefits that go into eating fruit.

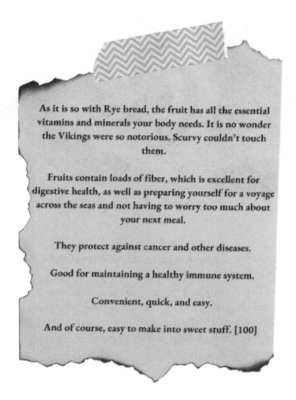

As it is so with Rye bread, the fruit has all the essential vitamins and minerals your body needs. It is no wonder the Vikings were so notorious. Scurvy couldn't touch them.

Fruits contain loads of fiber, which is excellent for digestive health, as well as preparing yourself for a voyage across the seas and not having to worry too much about your next meal.

They protect against cancer and other diseases.

Good for maintaining a healthy immune system.

Convenient, quick, and easy.

And of course, easy to make into sweet stuff. [100]

But what about the other sweet stuff? Well, nuts are another great source of lowering the risk of diseases, as said above. In fact, one of the oldest bodies ever found in Denmark had various nuts and berries in his belly! Pine, almond, and chestnuts can and does grow efficiently in Scandinavia, mainly Sweden and Denmark though, as they are warmer than Norway. Scandinavia doesn't always have the most fertile land, but the food that grows naturally is quite nutritious. In fact, modern Scandinavian dishes haven't forgotten about nuts. Almonds especially are a favorite in many traditional Scandinavian dishes.

Listed below are some more additional health benefits of nuts... [96]

They are loaded with antioxidants.

Excellent for eye and brain health.

Can aid significantly in weight loss.

Lower cholesterol and triglycerides.

Beneficial for type 2 diabetes.

Reduces inflammation.

High in fiber, which reduces the risk of stomach cancer.

Reduces the risk of a heart attack and/or stroke. [102]

Honey has more nutrients, minerals, antioxidants, and lowers the risk of diseases. [97]

Some more benefits to eating and drinking honey, and dairy, containing many nutrients and aid with the strengthening of bones. [98]...

Another excellent source of antioxidants.

It has antibacterial and antifungal properties.

Helps with your digestive issues.

Can aid a sore throat. [104]

The milk spectrum of the dairy scale is packed with nutrients, antioxidants, and omega fatty acids. All of which fight off disease.

Good source of high-quality protein which aids muscle repair.

Milk has loads of calcium and Vitamin D in it, which is very important for bone health and growth.

Stops you from putting on too many extra pounds, which you may end up needing for the holidays. [106]

An example of a traditional Norwegian dessert is the Krumkake. In Norwegian, this translates to "bent cake" and it is an indulgent treat that is so simple to create. It is a waffle-like cake, in a shape that is similar to an ice cream cone. This dessert has gained plenty of popularity in the other Scandinavian countries as well as Germany. To make it, you will need...

- A pizzelle iron to make the waffle cone, or you can purchase the cones pre-made.
- ½ cup of butter.
- ½ - 1 cup sugar.
- 2 eggs.
- 1 cup of milk (or non-dairy milk).
- 1 ½ cup of flour.
- ½ - 1 tsp of vanilla extract.

Serves: 2-4
Prep Time: 5 Minutes
Cooking Time: 3 Minutes

Here is how you go about it...

1. In a large bowl, add the eggs first, one each at a time, and mix until the consistency is thin. Then, add the vanilla, milk, and butter while thoroughly mixing.

2. If you have not bought the waffle cone premade, you can make it yourself. First, you will need a pizzelle iron. Place the mixed batter on the iron, and press it together. Cook for around 30 seconds on each side.

3. Remove the iron and quickly roll the iron or around a cone right before it hardens.

4. Once the cone hardens, add the sweetened cream inside the cone.

5. Add raw fruit on top if desired, such as berries, kiwi's, or even chocolate drizzle. [99]

The Nordic Method

Another traditional sweet dish is the Viking honey nut cake, prepared and eaten traditionally in all 3 Scandinavian countries.

Serves: 2-4
Prep Time: 5 Minutes
Cooking Time: 15 Minutes

What you'll need...

- 2 cups of hazelnuts.
- A cup of dried apple.
- 1 and a half cups of honey.
- 4 eggs.

Here is how you go about it...

1. Preheat your primitive clay oven to 350 degrees (175 Celsius). (Might take you a few attempts before you can guess that temperature without a thermometer).

2. Finely chop the hazelnuts with your homemade iron knife.

3. Mix the nuts, apple, and honey in your wooden bowl.

4. Whisk the eggs, spread the mixture onto your iron baking tray and bake for around 15 minutes in the middle of the oven. Again, you will need practice, without the modern-day stopwatch. [100]

Traditional Swedish pastries are typically made quite small, but boy are they memorable. You may be familiar with the cinnamon bun, vanilla custard pastry, and rhubarb cake, all of which are Swedish, but there is so much more than that. "Appelkaka" (apple pastry), "Pepparkakor" (Swedish ginger snap cookies, and "Ostkaka" (Swedish cheesecake) are all well-known pastries that hail from Sweden. Let's take a look at a lesser-known dessert; **The Praline Ice Cream Dessert**. [101]

Serves: 2-3
Prep Time: 10 Minutes
Cooking Time: 15 Minutes

What you'll need...

- 2 cups flour.
- ½ cup oats.
- ½ cup brown sugar.
- 1 cup melted butter.
- 1 cup chopped pecans.
- 12 ounces caramel topping.
- 3-4 cups vanilla ice cream.

Here is how you go about it...

1. Mix the first 5 ingredients in a bowl, and then spread evenly onto a baking sheet.

2. Bake at 400 degrees (200 Celsius) for 12-15 minutes.

3. Crumble the mix while warm.

4. Spread the crumbs onto a baking pan.

5. Pour half of the caramel topping on top of the crumble mix.

6. Spread softened ice cream over the caramel and crumble mix.

7. Add another layer of crumbs and add the remaining caramel topping.

8. Freeze until hardened and enjoy!

7

COOL SEA DIVIN'

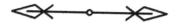

How the Nordic folk caught fish

It all started when the ice began to melt at the end of the ice age, and the Nordic folk had access to the waters around 10,000 years ago. [102]

Thanks to the open waters being something of an unknown territory, the Vikings kept to themselves and kept fishing strictly coastal (For the time being anyway). For the people residing more inland, fishing was kept more personal, and each household did so when they needed it. [102]

For those on the coast, however, fishing was a slightly bigger deal. Settlements were placed for that exact purpose. In summer times, the Nords would spend their time on agriculture by farming, but winter was a very different story. Those dry, cold, short days meant that vegetation couldn't survive. So it was up to the fishing culture to keep everyone's belly full. [102]

Enough about the why, you came here for the how and that is what we're going to get into shortly. The Vikings obviously used tools to make fishing more efficient. The traditional fish hook was used, made from iron. They used this to kill their enemies, so why not their food? Being resourceful in nature, they also made these hooks with bone for when Iron was not so freely available. [102]

The benefits and science behind the seafood

We all know that fish is brain food, but how else does seafood benefit our bodies? Well for starters, the oils from fish are so healthy that we have actually ended up making a multi-nutrient pill just made from fish oils called Omega-3. [103]

These fish oils are especially good for...

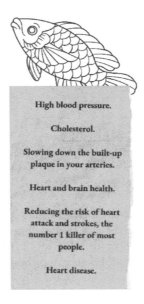

High blood pressure.

Cholesterol.

Slowing down the built-up plaque in your arteries.

Heart and brain health.

Reducing the risk of heart attack and strokes, the number 1 killer of most people.

Heart disease.

Vikings and other Nordic folk spent a large amount of their time on the ocean, so it only makes sense that they took full use of this. We know that fish was consumed quite often, but there was far more than just fish to feast on. Common seafood animals that the Vikings ate included...

Whale.

Shellfish.

OCTOPUS.

SHARK.

Prawns.

Vikings didn't hunt whales often, but it did occur due to certain types of whales swimming slowly and sometimes in shallow water. This made them an easy target when food was sparse. But whale meat was abundant and could feed many families while also providing many nutrients. Whale meat is certainly not a common dish in modern times, and most countries even ban whale hunting to preserve this species. However, the capture of prawns, lobster, octopus, and other fish was more common in ancient

Scandinavia.

Algae

Algae has to be on your hypothetical 3 things you would take if you were trapped on a remote island, with no food or people, in the middle of space. [104]

Basically, all of sea life has Algae to thank for not going extinct during the past one million years. Algae only need energy from sunlight to give off everything people need to survive.

Algae make these food molecules from carbon dioxide and water through photosynthesis. The human race also needs to take a moment to thank Algae for making up 30 to 50 percent of the global oxygen we use. [104]

Kelp

The third and final addition to our nutrient-packed sea life cuisine would have to be kelp. Kelp is the healthy strain of seaweed that you can ingest, and seaweed is a type of algae. It is a sea vegetable and the largest one at that, essentially a superfood and a brown seaweed that grows in salty, nutrient-rich seawater. It is estimated that kelp has been in our oceans for millions of years. There are even 30 different types of kelp in our ocean, each with unique and beneficial purposes and benefits. Kelp loves and grows from sunlight, even though it also thrives and grows in the cold and salty Atlantic water, all around Scandinavia. Kelp can grow to enormous lengths, with some species of kelp growing up to 135 feet (40 meters)!

Luckily, kelp is not hard to find and normally grows as a dense thick forest in the ocean. [105,106]

Kelp is not only consumed by humans, but many other animals need kelp and seaweed for food and even shelter in the ocean, sometimes hiding from predators in this thick kelp forest.

In addition to all the vitamins, minerals, and iodine kelp contain, it has also been shown to boost energy levels and brain function. Kelp has also shown great promise in fighting diseases and helping greatly with weight loss. [105]

Kelp even has specific benefits for women, hormones, and fertility. Kelp and seaweed contain iodine, which can directly positively affect thyroid function in women with hypothyroidism. Many women have been known to take kelp as a supplement to treat hypothyroidism, rather than risky prescription medication that tends to have horrible side effects. Kelp can aid the body in cleaning out the blood and removing certain toxins. Painful hormonal conditions in women such as endometriosis, PCOS, and uterine fibroids directly negatively affect fertility. This is because these conditions run on excess estrogen in a woman's blood. When kelp is eaten or taken as a supplement, it removes the "bad" estrogen and excess estrogen, and therefore it helps to heal these conditions naturally. Kelp and seaweed contain over 60 trace elements and even packs in more calcium than dairy and milk! What makes kelp such an efficient disease fighter, is the high content of antioxidants, minerals, and flavonoids. Flavonoids destroy harmful agents and free radicals in our bodies. Kelp has an enormous amount of benefits, frankly too many to name, but the main benefits are...

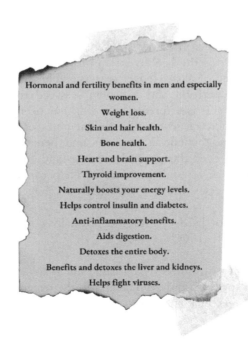

Hormonal and fertility benefits in men and especially women.

Weight loss.

Skin and hair health.

Bone health.

Heart and brain support.

Thyroid improvement.

Naturally boosts your energy levels.

Helps control insulin and diabetes.

Anti-inflammatory benefits.

Aids digestion.

Detoxes the entire body.

Benefits and detoxes the liver and kidneys.

Helps fight viruses.

As you can see, kelp is an absolute superfood that the ancient Nords consumed quite often, and even to this day, it is still consumed. Kelp is quite low in calories, so feel free to add plenty to your meal! Some popular kelp/seaweed dishes in Scandinavia now are...

Seaweed soup.

SEAWEED RISOTTO.

Seaweed salad.

SEAWEED PESTO.

Seaweed tartare.

SEAWEED CHIPS.

Seaweed pizza.

Most seaweed is prepared by boiling, cooking, or frying. Most will also choose to soak their seaweed in water before cooking it, to remove the salty taste. Kelp can be blended into a sauce or pesto as well. Seaweed can also be dried and eaten as crisps for a snack. This is a versatile and healthy additive that many Scandinavian dishes are made up of.

The Nordic method

How the Scandinavians won over the sea...

Unlike many other cultures, wanting to colonize for expansion, the Viking people colonized other lands purely out of economic interest. [107]

The Viking people basically lived on the sea and had to conform to a predominantly seafood diet. They colonized countries throughout Europe, and eventually made it all the way to North America, beating Christopher Columbus by about 500 years. [108]

How Scandinavians cooked their fish

A very popular dish in Scandinavian culture is the Lutefisk. Lutefisk, pronounced LEWD-A-FISK is a dried Codfish that soaks in a lye solution for several days to rehydrate it. The excess lye is then rinsed off with cold water. The rehydrated fish is then either boiled or baked, and usually served with butter, salt, and pepper. [109]

Normally fish was soaked in lye for the pure purpose of preservation. [110] Of course, as it was with smoked food, Lutefisk is still enjoyed today for the taste, and the cultural nature associated with it. The finished meal has a jelly-like consistency. It's one of those meals that you either love or hate, but even then, most agree that enjoying this Scandinavian delicacy once a year is quite enough.

There are many legends as to why Lutefisk became a delicacy to the Vikings. Some say that the Irish poisoned the Viking fish barrels with lye, but the Vikings ended up enjoying it. Other legends say that after burning down a fishing village, along with the drying racks with cod, returning villagers poured water on the flames to put it out. Ashes covered the dried fish, and then it rained. The fish buried in the ash eventually became soaked in the lye slush that the ash had turned into. The villagers were surprised to see that the dried fish seemed to look like fresh fish. They rinsed the fish off in the river and boiled it, waiting for one brave soul to eventually go and try it, to which he replied it was "not bad". [109]

There are many legend stories about the origin of the Lutefisk, and we will never know if any of them are true... What we do know to be true, is why this tradition was kept over the years. That is because drying out the fish kept it preserved and the lye was used as nutrition. The science behind it, which we only could find out in modern times, is that the lye breaks down the protein in the fish to amino acids. These amino acids are easily absorbed by the intestine. [111]

The modern approach to seafood

The modern Scandinavian diet still incorporates a lot of fish into their meals, however, it is more presentable and easier to make nowadays. There is also the fact that after centuries of perfecting and trying all kinds of different types of combinations, the variety of how one goes about eating the infamous codfish is limitless.

One of these interesting Norwegian recipes comes from a recipe of food.com. This is oven-baked cod with lemon or "ovnsstekt torsk med sitron" in Norwegian.

What you need

1 pound (Half a kilogram) of cod fillet.

¼ cup (2.5 fl oz) of melted butter.

2 tablespoons of lemon juice.

¼ cup (2.5 fl oz) of flour.

½ teaspoon of salt.

1/8 teaspoon of white pepper.

Paprika.

How to make

First, preheat the oven to 350 degrees F (175 Celsius).

Cut the cod into preferred serving-size pieces.

Mix the butter and lemon juice together.

In a separate bowl, mix together the flour, salt, and white pepper.

.Dip the codpieces into the butter and lemon mixture, then roll it around in the flour mixture.

Place the codpieces into an 8 x 8" pan, then pour whatever is left of the butter mixture on top. Sprinkle a bit of paprika on top.

Bake uncovered for about 25 to 30 minutes.

Finish it off by garnishing the dish with lemon slices and freshly chopped parsley. [120]

Types of fish in Northern waters

Due to the commercialization of fish, numbers are dropping at a rapid rate due to overfishing. Sadly, the Houtingfish is now extinct. All the other types of fish that can survive in the Northern waters can still be found there. There is a long list of possible fish, so we'll only list a few...

It's really no secret that Scandinavians love their seafood and it is very much ingrained in their culture to this day, with at least one meal per day having some sort of seafood in it. The Swedes are no exception and many of their traditional classic dishes are seafood dishes (surströmming anyone?). Something a bit more fresh and tasty though would be Toast Skagen (prawns/shrimp on toast). This is a quick and simple lunch recipe that is just too delicious to pass on, and the best part is that you can make this quickly at home. The name Skagen is actually a town in Denmark, although this dish is actually known as a Swedish dish. You will see that there typically is a lot of overlap between Denmark, Norway, and Sweden in many ways, including food and recipes.

Let's take a look at how to make the **"Toast Skagen"** aka Skagenröra!

Serves: 1-2
Prep/Cook Time: 10 Minutes

You will need...

- Shrimp or prawns, your choice.
- 4 tbsp Mayonnaise.
- 4 tbsp Sour Cream.
- 2 tbsp dill.
- 2 tbsp chives.
- Bread slices.
- Pinch of salt & pepper.
- Butter for the bread.
- Lemon wedge.

Here is how you go about it...

1. Shell the prawns and keep them at a cool temperature.

2. In a bowl, mix the cold sour cream, mayonnaise, chives, and dill. If it becomes warm or room temperature, place it in the fridge until ready to be served.

3. Toast your bread slices, and spread butter on them while warm so that it melts.

4. Spread the cool sour cream and mayonnaise mix on your bread, and garnish with pepper and a lemon wedge.

5. Serve and enjoy! [112]

As you can see, this is a delicious Swedish lunch recipe that you can make in no time! I highly recommend it.

Another simple lunch/dinner recipe is the Danish Fiskefrikadeller (Fish balls/patties). This is a twist on the Swedish meatballs, but it uses fish and seafood rather than beef or pork. This dish may have been created by using leftover fish and other ingredients. "Fiskefrikadeller" is usually served with a sauce, ideally remoulade or another cream-based sauce. We will use remoulade for this recipe.

Serves: 1-3
Prep Time: 5 Minutes
Cooking Time: 10-15 Minutes

Here's what you'll need...

- Your choice of minced fish or seafood.
- 1 egg.
- 3 tbsp flour.
- 1/2 cup (5 fl oz) of cream.
- 2 tbsp of dill.
- 1 diced onion.
- 2 cloves of garlic.

- 1 cup (10 fl oz) of breadcrumbs (optional - only if you want to add some crispiness).
- 2 tbsp butter or olive oil for frying.
- Pinch of salt & pepper.

For the remoulade sauce...

- 1 cup (10 fl oz) mayonnaise.
- 2 tbsp of dill.
- 1 tbsp lemon juice.
- 2 tsp of parsley.
- 1-2 tbsp of mustard.
- Pinch of salt & pepper.

Here is how you go about it...

1. Use a food processor to grind your fish until it is minced finely.

2. Slowly add the egg, flour, garlic, cream one at a time and grind slowly until all ingredients are combined thoroughly.

3. Form the batter into small patty shapes with or without adding breadcrumbs, and fry on a heated pan with olive oil or butter.

4. Fry until golden brown on both sides.

5. Combine the remoulade ingredients in a bowl until a smooth and creamy texture, and refrigerate while the Fiskefrikadeller is cooking.

6. Serve and enjoy!

Traditionally, "fiskefrikadeller" is served with baked or boiled potatoes and your choice of veggies on the side. But feel free to eat pasta or rice with it for example!

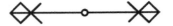

Ancient Scandinavians were resourceful folk, they had to be. Living in freezing climates, not many survived. One thing they did enjoy indulging themselves in was meat. They pretty much ate anything they could get their hands on, whether it be beef or pork, or even horse meat. [113,114]

You can imagine that this annoyed a lot of people, especially the Christian people who believed that eating horse meat was a common pagan practice.

Even though the Vikings ate a lot of "taboo" meat, they stayed away from the cat and the dog. Ancient drawings suggest that the Viking folk loved the cat and dog so much, that they were thought to accompany their masters to the afterlife. One such depiction was of Freja riding in a chariot pulled by her cats and dogs into the afterlife. [113]

The cows, goats, and sheep, however, weren't slaughtered immediately. Instead, they were only slaughtered after they stopped giving milk or wool. If that isn't motivation to keep supplying milk, then I don't know what is. [113]

Let's not forget all the seafood they had in their diet thanks to their many years at sea. [114]

How was meat prepared?

Contrary to popular belief, the Viking method of cooking meat was not so much roasted, as much as it was boiled. [113,114]

They did this because instead of setting up a whole new system each time they wanted to cook food when roasting, the boiling method proved to be a lot simpler and tastier.

The Vikings would just add new meat to the pot when needed and take out the cooked meat when it was ready to be eaten. Not only did this make things easier, but it helped a lot in the way of flavoring food. This process also allowed them to add all sorts of other food to the pot such as vegetables, turning whatever they ate into a super flavored stew. The broth from cooking would sit in the pot for sometimes days. [114]

The health benefits and science behind Nordic meat

Firstly, we're going to touch on the nutritional benefits of boiling meat and other food.

Basically, when it comes to nutrients, it all depends on what you do with the water and stew leftover. This is because when you boil meat, all the nutrients and good stuff our body loves so much are seeped out into the water. Throwing that broth onto some tasty Scandinavian rye bread for example, may be the best way to enjoy those delicious nutrients. [115]

Beef

Beef is a type of meat loved by all nations, and the Scandinavian folk was no exception. In the three languages, beef is storfekjøtt in Norwegian, nötkött in Swedish, and "oksekød" in Danish. Although they only slaughtered the cow after they had served their milk giving uses. [116]

Benefits of beef...

HIGHLY RICH IN PROTEIN, WHICH HELPS MUSCLE GROWTH AND MUSCLE MASS.

INCLUDES THE FOUR VITAMINS OF THE ESSENTIAL DIET INCLUDING NIACIN, RIBOFLAVIN, VITAMINS B6 AND B12.

BEEF IS ALSO A RICH SOURCE OF ZINC, WHICH IS INCREDIBLE FOR YOUR HAIR, NAILS, AND SKIN. IT ALSO ENSURES THAT YOU WILL HAVE LITTLE VERSIONS OF YOURSELF RUNNING AROUND ONE DAY BY PROMOTING FERTILITY, REPRODUCTION, AND HORMONE STABILITY.

YOU CAN ALSO THANK THE IRON IN BEEF, ESSENTIAL FOR KEEPING A GREAT IMMUNE SYSTEM.

Duck

The duck was absolutely eaten by the ancient Nordic folk. It is not as popular as other traditional meat nowadays. However, it is surprisingly nutritious meat. Duck meat is packed full of protein, in fact, duck contains more protein than even chicken. Duck also tends to have a stronger flavor than other meat and is most commonly consumed today in China, the USA, and France.

Let's look at the benefits below...

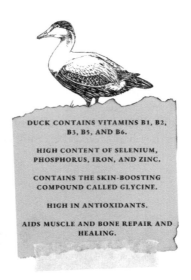

DUCK CONTAINS VITAMINS B1, B2, B3, B5, AND B6.

HIGH CONTENT OF SELENIUM, PHOSPHORUS, IRON, AND ZINC.

CONTAINS THE SKIN-BOOSTING COMPOUND CALLED GLYCINE.

HIGH IN ANTIOXIDANTS.

AIDS MUSCLE AND BONE REPAIR AND HEALING.

Pork

The infamous pork food group. Taboo by various religions, yet the bacon is irresistible to many. For those of you that want to find excuses to eat more pork or maybe you just want to follow the Viking way, we are going to list some excuses you can use below...

PORK MEAT IS PACKED WITH OVER 10
KINDS OF VITAMINS, ESPECIALLY VITAMIN
B.

IT IS HIGH IN PROTEIN WHICH AIDS IN
MUSCLE GROWTH AND MAINTENANCE (A
DEFINITE REQUIREMENT FOR THE VIKING
FOLK).

IT ALSO ASSISTS IN YOUR ABILITY TO
CONDUCT THE WORKOUTS AND EXERCISES
THAT YOU WANT BY UPPING YOUR
EVERYDAY PERFORMANCE. [126,127]

PORK IS EQUALLY AS HEALTHY FOR YOU AS
LEAN CHICKEN.

When some think of Swedish food, you likely think of Swedish meatballs, as this is a well-known recipe all over the world. However, there is another famous Swedish recipe that not too many non-Swedes are aware of. Äppelfläsk, meaning "apple pork" in Swedish, is a traditional recipe that consists of pork, apples, spices, and onions. The average Swede consumes roughly 53 lbs (24 kg) of pork in just 1 year! [117]

The Swedes can't get enough pork! This dish is from the area of Skåne in Southern Sweden. Pork and fruit may seem like an odd combination, but it somehow works and is quite delicious and compatible. The fruit is sweet, while the pork is salty and savory. Let's take a look at the recipe, you will need...

- 7-10 oz of lean pork.
- 2-3 green or red apples.
- 1-2 onions.
- A pinch of ginger.
- Olive oil for frying.
- Spices of your choice.

Here is what you will have to do...

1. Start with oiling your pan and placing it on medium heat. Place your pork on the pan and cook until golden and crispy.

2. Cut apples into wedges as well as the onions.

3. Add the onions and apples to the pan with the pork.

4. Fry until golden, or until desired consistency is met.
5. Add the pinch of ginger.

6. Spoon any juices from the pan and add to the plate.

7. Serve and enjoy!

Reindeer

Reindeer are plentiful in Norway, and even the meat is often sold in grocery stores and restaurants. Reindeer has a distinct taste and is described as lean and mild. Hunting reindeer has long been normalized in countries such as Norway, Sweden, and Finland. Ancient Scandinavians would hunt reindeers for their fur, antlers, milk, and meat. They had many important uses in Norway, and they were also used to pull sleds and carts as they were domesticated and trainable, unlike the traditional deer.

To no surprise, reindeer meat is very nutritious with plenty of benefits. One of the main reasons why many believe reindeer are so healthy is because they feed on nutritious grass and greens all day. Take a look at the breakdown of this Nordic meat...

REINDEER HAS NEARLY AS MUCH OMEGA-3S AND OMEGA-6S AS SEAFOOD! [129]

LOW IN FAT AND IS LEAN AND HEALTHY MEAT, RATHER THAN FATTY.

LOWERS CHOLESTEROL IN YOUR BLOOD.

CARBOHYDRATE-FREE AND LOW SODIUM.

FULL OF PHOSPHORUS, IRON, POTASSIUM, ZINC, B6 & B12, RIBOFLAVIN, THIAMIN, AND NIACIN.

RICH IN NATURAL PROTEIN.

CONTAINS PLENTY OF FATTY ACIDS WHICH REDUCE INFLAMMATION IN YOUR BODY.

REINDEER MILK CONTAINS FAR MORE NATURAL PROTEIN THAN COW'S MILK.

REINDEER MILK IS OFTEN USED IN ANTI-AGING MOISTURIZING CREAMS.

PACKED FULL OF B12, WHICH HELPS KEEP YOUR CELLS HEALTHY.

Let's cook a traditional Norwegian reindeer dish! "Dyrestek med viltsaus" is a reindeer dish with game sauce. It is a delicious recipe that is quite simple to make.

HERE'S WHAT YOU'LL NEED...

Reindeer meat. (choose your serving size)

1/2 cup of milk.

3 tbsp of butter.

Suet (fat) from the reindeer.

Seasonings of your choice (salt, pepper, oregano, parsley is recommended).

Red currant jam.

Sour cream.

Flour.

Goat cheese.

Tomatoes.

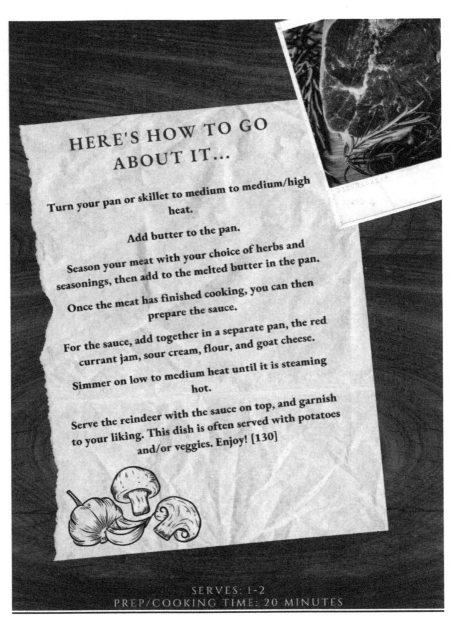

HERE'S HOW TO GO ABOUT IT...

Turn your pan or skillet to medium to medium/high heat.

Add butter to the pan.

Season your meat with your choice of herbs and seasonings, then add to the melted butter in the pan.

Once the meat has finished cooking, you can then prepare the sauce.

For the sauce, add together in a separate pan, the red currant jam, sour cream, flour, and goat cheese.

Simmer on low to medium heat until it is steaming hot.

Serve the reindeer with the sauce on top, and garnish to your liking. This dish is often served with potatoes and/or veggies. Enjoy! [130]

SERVES: 1-2
PREP/COOKING TIME: 20 MINUTES

The not so well accepted horse meat

In no way are we saying you should go out and source horse meat in this section, this is purely educational and an explanation as to why the Viking would occasionally eat this type of meat. Horse meat is illegal in most countries in our modern-day.

Toxicity of horse meat.

In a socially responsible effort to further your plans away from trying out the unconventional horse meat. We are first and foremost going to tell you why it is such a horrible idea.

At the top of the list is the fact that for centuries, horses have not been bred for consumption. Livestock such as cows, on the other hand, have. For that reason, they have been conditioned over generations for such a purpose. Horses have been bred for transport in the olden days and injected with substances and trained for racing in modern times. This means that toxicity levels of horse meat can be very high, and several outbreaks have been recorded in countries that allow horse meat for consumption. [118]

Now as for the nutritional benefits horse meat may have offered in the olden days... [119]

- Horse meat had less fat and cholesterol than other meat.
- It assisted in helping with asthma.
- Improved your immune system.
- Horse meat helped strengthen your bones.
- It assisted in muscular growth.
- Improved levels of stamina.

Before moving onto the next section, we'd like to take a moment to stress how not ok it is to eat your pet horse like the Vikings may have done in history. Times have changed, and things are very different now. For instance, we resolve conflict through mediation or even through a court of law... not by fighting with swords.

The Nordic method

Why did the Vikings eat horse meat?

Horse meat became popular in the pagan Viking times. [120] Horses were not normally consumed, as they were expensive and thought of as a prized possession.

They were usually consumed when praising the pagan gods such as Odin, Thor, and the likes. [121]

This was because the horse was associated with high status, special occasions, and even how warriors may have been transported to the afterlife... like Valhalla. [122]

So when the time of the Christians came, horse meat was associated with pagan practices and banned in Christian culture. Of course, this caused quite a bit of conflict within the Viking community, and even one of the kings was highly conflicted. Thomas Roswell reads from a Viking book written in the 13th century of a Christian Viking King trying to lead his people, but also avoid going to hell from eating the taboo meat.

9

RYE IS FLY

Bread has always been a part of most culture's diets. The earliest evidence of bread being used dates back to somewhere around 12,000 BCE in the desert region of modern-day Jordan. However, grinding stones for such bread can be traced back as far as 30,000 years ago from today. [123]

The bread was first used on a mass scale in Ancient Egypt. The miracle of bread had shown that the masses could be fed, giving them more than enough energy to carry out strenuous activities. Activities such as slaves having to build the Pyramids. While it also meant that families could get bigger and be sustained. This meant population sizes exploded, and it created ever more establishments. What this meant was those specialist roles needed other specialist roles, such as soldiers protecting these vast numbers of people. There is a running theory that food availability and the production thereof lead to greater numbers of people, which leads to food storage. Some people residing over more food than others exerted control over many others and created means to protect and organize these storages. Essentially whole nations were built up due to food availability, and the discovery of bread was paramount in this development. [124] This is also why today that the vast majority of food is with either wheat, corn, potatoes, rice, or soy. A very limiting diet as opposed to our ancestors of hunter-gatherers. Which you know all about now from reading, "What Lurks in the Forest". [125,126]

The bread had made its way through the times until it finally made its popularity in the Nordic countries in 500 CE, making it the staple diet of the people of Scandinavia. [127]

The bread was then moved onto other areas through the ages as well. It was used to feed hundreds of thousands of soldiers to fight in wars, as can be seen throughout Roman times. The bread was also used in these times to keep the masses happy when not being entertained by fighting gladiators. Romans, for example, used to give 75-pounds of bread to each and every household. All to prevent the Roman populous from starting an uprising… which, actually worked. [126,128]

As bread became more and more popular, different and cheaper ways were discovered by famous chemists to make bread until eventually, baking powder became a household name. When this happened, people accepted that this was as good as it was going to get. Until the invention that seems deceptively simple came into existence; sliced bread. Before baker's sliced the bread at the point of sale, this would keep the freshness of the bread itself and wouldn't require any preservatives to not go stale immediately. But it immediately struck a chord with consumers and soared in sales. While rolling carts were filled with the new wonder bread, bakers were more than just biffed and thought of it as yet another "roaring twenties" fad - like jazz dancing. But it did take off and eventually arrived at the shores of the North. But with it many preservatives, some banned in the EU and there in the North as well. Preservatives such as Azodicarbonamide (ACA) are used to lighten the sliced bread. This substance has been seen to cause cancer in animals. Or the other chemical Potassium bromate which aids the bread to rise more quickly and makes the production of bread more effective has been linked with kidney and thyroid cancer in rodents. [128,129]

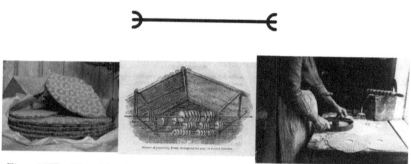

Figure 66 TL; Slices of knäckebröd, M; conservation of the knäckebröd, TR; 1911 traditional

But let's move on to some more pleasant topics.

In Sweden, a popular bread variant is called "knäckebröd or hårt bröd", see figure 16 to the left. This is translated to 'crisp or hard bread' in English. A big Swedish bread company that sells its crispy goodies to the other Nordic countries and Germany is Wasa, which has been making knäckebröd since 1919. [130] Crispbread is primarily made with rye flour and is made into these thin but hard-baked, crispy, slices of bread. It almost resembles that of a cracker. Historically knäckebröd was considered a poor person's food, due to its longer spoiling period - see figure 16 again, to the right. In the past, it was a continual struggle to find ways to preserve food being made, using that of burying them down beneath the ground, smoking, salting, or drying. Or in this case, overly bake the bread to create knäckebröd, and then dry it after just beneath the ceiling - see in the middle of figure 16. See, it has been found that since 500 CE, that knäckebröd have been baked in families as their special variant of bread. Then it was a simple recipe with just three things; wholemeal rye flour, salt, and water. Today you will find variants with all manner of seeds to accompany and liven the taste up. Although, as a person who ate crispbread throughout their childhood, the taste experience is simple. But rewarding, and many use this in the same way the open-faced sandwich is made. So with a healthy assortment of toppings, there are many variants for your tastebuds.

Let's go into the more positive angle of looking at fresh natural bread's benefits.

The benefits and science behind why bread is such a wonder.

Scandinavians originally started their love for rye bread because of location. Just as the Japanese became famous for their sushi and the Irish became famous for their potatoes. Something called the Rye belt stretches from Germany to Russia, passing through the Nordic countries can be thanked for making rye bread in Scandinavia so popular. Integrating this food into their cultural dishes and delicacies was becoming normal. [131]

Rye bread typically has that stronger, earthier taste than white bread. Many different variations of Rye bread can be made, which is also a healthier alternative to other bread. It has been linked to health benefits like weight loss, reduced inflammation, a more controlled blood sugar level, and better health for digestion and your heart. [131–133]

The full nutritional profile can be found below.

Per 32 grams of Rye bread

- 83 kcal.
- 2.7 grams of protein.
- 15.5 grams of carbohydrates.
- 1.1 grams of fat.
- 1.9 grams of fiber.

As well as trace amounts of all the good vitamins and nutrients such as Selenium, Thiamine, Manganese and much other good stuff you may read on your 1-a-day bottle of vitamins. [134]

Rye bread is also extremely high in fiber, so it can drop your LDL cholesterol, or the bad cholesterol levels significantly, and therefore drop your risk of horrible heart disease significantly. [134] The science behind this, is the high soluble fiber content in the bread. This indigestible fiber forms a gel-like substance that sits in your digestive tract collecting all the unhealthy cholesterol dominant bile from your blood and body, making rye bread a lot healthier than its white and wheat bread cousins. [133]

The gel that comes from the soluble fiber in your digestive tract can also be thanked for aiding in proper blood sugar control. This is because that gel slows down digestion, and absorption of carbs and sugars. This process is how weight loss is aided because slower digestion means feeling fuller for longer. [133]

Rye bread is also a wonderful source of micronutrients, aka compounds that are only needed in tiny doses to assist in the growth and maintenance of a healthy body. [134] Other compounds found in rye bread include bioactive and phenolic compounds. Bioactive compounds are substances that can modulate one or more metabolic processes. These processes are what your body goes through when converting food into energy, in essence, meaning that better metabolic processes mean a better and healthier lifestyle. [133]

Phenolic compounds are full of all the anti-bad stuff. Antioxidants, antivirals, anticancer, and anti-inflammatory. [133]

The Nordic Method.

As mentioned before, the love of Rye bread for the Scandinavian culture was born because of location. [131] But when did all of this occur? Why? And of course, how? Four kinds of grains were dominant in Nordic countries throughout their history. Barley, rye, wheat, and oats. The rise of the Rye came about in the iron age, 500 – 1050 AD, a time when rye was the most commonly used grain. Rye would continue on being the most commonly used grain all the way up until the early 20th century. [127]

Now that 'the when' is established, 'the why' is the next question. The Vikings believed that this strain of grain granted them copious levels of strength to aid them in battle. [135]

This can be seen by the scientific evidence today of how many nutrients are in Rye bread. Rye was not only used in bread but in porridge as well. [135]

Finally, for the how. Nordic countries used their resources properly and had a wide variety of resources they could use. Their farming of rye grain was possible by the use of a moldboard plow, which could even be used on poor soil. [136]

Now vs then, today's meals compared to the ancient recipes.

During the time of the Vikings, bread was baked using the hearthstone. [137]

Flat plates with long shafts were held over open embers. [138] The higher up you were in terms of importance, the finer the bread was that you ate. Flat grain bread was used as a plate to eat off, making a tasty snack afterward. This plate was soaked with the juices and sauces that came from the meal just eaten. [127]

To make the journey of cooking rye bread in ancient times, and for those who just want to taste the meal, I have listed both ways in how you can go about making Rye bread.

The old-fashioned way of making rugbrød (rye bread).

Figure 77 Homemade ryebread, Public Domain

See what your finished result will look like by taking a gander up at figure 17.

Firstly, some starter dough is needed, and we'll tell you exactly how to make that if you are fresh out of the stuff. You'll need...

- One pinch of fresh yeast.
- 300 ml of water.
- 300 ml of Rye flour.

Dissolve the yeast in water and mix it in with the flour. You should end up with a loose porridge-type consistency. Leave overnight for fermentation, at room temperature covered by a linen cloth. The starter will be ready to be used when it starts bubbling on top.

Secondly, you'll need to do what's called scalding. Here's what you'll need to get that right...

- 200 ml of crushed smoked barley. (You can use normal barley if you can't find the smoked stuff).
- 400 ml of water at 150 degrees Fahrenheit (66 degrees Celsius).

Of course, nobody had thermometers in those times, the only experience in telling them what the right temperature was and when to do it. As you may not be an experienced Viking, we suggest you use some of the tools of the 21st century.

First, let the barley malt steep in the warm 150-degree water. Be sure to keep the temperature around 140 and 150 degrees for around half an hour to convert most of the starch to sugar. When that's done, raise the temperature to 200 degrees. You may need practice with this step if you're not using modern methods and doing it over the fire. When you get that right, let the mixture stand until the grains are soft and like porridge. Then, as you do with the starter dough, let it rest overnight for 8 to 10 hours at room temperature and covered by a linen cloth.

Finally, the last step, the dough. Here's what you'll need for the final part of your plan.

- Your starter dough.
- The scalded barley.
- 400 ml of whey.
- 600 ml of rye flour.
- Around 1200 ml of wheat flour.
- 1 tbsp of table salt.

Start by mixing the starter, the barley, whey, rye flour, and salt if you decided to go with it. Add the wheat flour bit by bit until you come across the right texture. Work the dough thoroughly by hand for around 10 minutes. Then go attend to your other Nordic matters while you wait for the dough to rise, around 3 to 4 hours at room temperature, covered by a damp linen cloth. The bread will be ready when it has doubled in size.

If you're using the apparatus the 21st century has blessed us with, preheat to 400 degrees (200 Celsius), while leaving the baking stone or metal baking tray inside to heat along with it. Go ahead and divide the dough into 24 pieces and roll them out into small buns. Then roll the buns in some flour and leave it to rise further for another 40 minutes, while covered.

Finish up the preparation by cutting an "X" on top of the buns with a sharp knife. When that's done, put the rolls onto the heated baking stone or baking tray inside your modern or traditional oven. Bake until they have a nice brownish color, which takes around 40 minutes. Take the freshly baked delicious rye, wrap them in a linen cloth and they should last a few days.

The modern method.

The quickest way to get rye bread on your table isn't the freshest. For this method, you will need a form of your local currency, mode of transportation, and a local bakery. However, you can use the modern tools to bake rye bread from scratch, if you don't want to just buy from the store.

Most of the ingredients and processes are extremely similar to the way of the ancestors, just done in a lot less time with a lot less hassle. For starters, the total time needed for the modern method is 70 minutes max. Preparation takes 30 minutes and baking takes 40 minutes. [139]

For starters, you'll need...

- 2 packs of active dry yeast (about 4 and a half teaspoons).
- 2.5 cups of warm water.
- 2/3 cup of molasses.
- 2 tablespoons of caraway seeds.
- 1 tablespoon of salt.
- ¼ cup of vegetable oil.
- ¼ cup of cocoa powder.
- 2 cups of rye flour.
- 5 cups of bread flour.

Now for the steps...

1. Throw the yeast and molasses together into warm water, and allow for the yeast to dissolve. Then transfer the mixture into a large metal bowl.

2. Now go ahead and throw the rest of the ingredients in, one at a time, mixing each ingredient into the mixture. But, be stingy on the bread flour.... You'll only need about 2 cups of this.

3. Add the bread flour one cup at a time, still mixing with each addition until the dough isn't as sticky and it is hard to mix with your wooden spoon.

4. When you get here, throw half a cup of bread flour onto a large, flat, and most importantly clean surface for you to put the dough onto.

5. Now is when you need to put in a little elbow grease. Knead the dough by pressing down with the heel of your hand, stretching and turning the dough a quarter turn, then pulling the dough back to you, then doing it all over again.

6. Knead additional flour into the dough until the consistency is just right. Keep kneading for 5 to 7 minutes, until the dough reaches smooth elasticity.

7. Sprinkle some vegetable dough into a large bowl, then place the dough inside, turning it over and over until it is covered in the oil.

8. Cover the bowl with plastic wrap, or a damp cloth and wait for the dough to be all it can be, and rise over the next 1 to 1 ½ hours.

9. When the dough has reached its full potential, gently press down on it to release some of the air. Place the dough on a lightly floured surface, and do a little more kneading, just a few times. Divide it up by cutting it in the middle with a sharp knife.

10. Shape the loaves, in whatever fancy bread dishes you may have. Note that you can add chocolate into the dough to bake your bread sweeter and the dark sour chocolate adds a wonderful dimension to the bread - you should try it. It is taking off in Scandinavia right now with adding 70% dark chocolate to the mix.

11. Allow the dough to become overachievers and rise that little bit more, you'll need to give it about 30 to 45 minutes.

12. Preheat the oven to 350 degrees (180 degrees Celsius)

13. Put the dough into the oven for baking, mist it with water if you can for the first 10 minutes. The whole process should take around 40 to 50 minutes… but keep an eye out just in case.

14. Eat and be merry! [139]

Rye bread chips, the modern snack you will see everywhere in the stores nowadays.

If you travel to one of the Scandinavian countries today, then you will see in bakeries and grocery stores placed strategically, front and center, rye bread chips right in front of you. Some will have fancy product designs and branding of "Garlic to keep the Viking vampires away" or "Fire in your mouth chili". The United States has had these hard-baked and roasted rye chips for a long time. But it is beginning now to become a healthy trend of snacking in Scandinavia. Used as a remedy, keeping yourself afloat until dinner time. There is even a growing variant that is a regular in every café, chain, and independent, and that is the chocolate rye bread buns. I will show you how to make both.

The freshly baked rye bread you made from the recipe just above.

Olive oil, or any other oil you will like better.

Some salt amounts depending on your sensitivity to sodium.

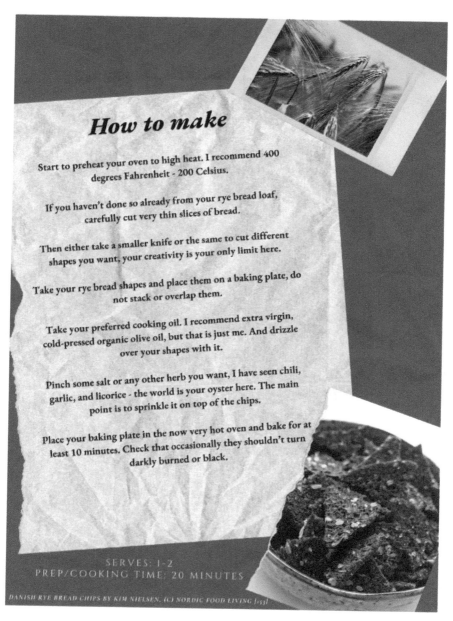

How to make

Start to preheat your oven to high heat. I recommend 400 degrees Fahrenheit - 200 Celsius.

If you haven't done so already from your rye bread loaf, carefully cut very thin slices of bread.

Then either take a smaller knife or the same to cut different shapes you want, your creativity is your only limit here.

Take your rye bread shapes and place them on a baking plate, do not stack or overlap them.

Take your preferred cooking oil. I recommend extra virgin, cold-pressed organic olive oil, but that is just me. And drizzle over your shapes with it.

Pinch some salt or any other herb you want, I have seen chili, garlic, and licorice - the world is your oyster here. The main point is to sprinkle it on top of the chips.

Place your baking plate in the now very hot oven and bake for at least 10 minutes. Check that occasionally they shouldn't turn darkly burned or black.

SERVES: 1-2
PREP/COOKING TIME: 20 MINUTES

DANISH RYE BREAD CHIPS BY KIM NIELSEN, (C) NORDIC FOOD LIVING [55]

10

A TYPICAL SCANDINAVIAN GARDEN

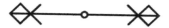

History

Compared to Southern countries, ancient Scandinavia didn't have as many options for food. But the food that does grow naturally in Scandinavia was enough to sustain its residents. Even had many rich nutritional benefits. The Berries, Roots, wheat, potatoes, herbs, onions, apples, and cherries are just a few examples of healthy food that grows naturally in Scandinavia. And by extension, in the Scandinavian garden.

Since the era of the Vikings, the ancient Nords knew their land and exactly how to cultivate the available food. This allowed them to thrive and grow in population, despite the harsh and prolonged winters. The native people would use the ocean, forests, marshlands, coastal areas, and rivers as a source for produce. In fact, almost all Scandinavian men worked as farmers to feed their families, and they were competent because they knew their lives depended on it. Food was scarce in the winter and late fall, and the Nords knew that preparation and saving of food was essential to survive. Luckily, most grains were easy to save and store as they did not require any special preservation, and they could be eaten months or even years later. Produce has a propensity for spoiling, and we will get into how the Northerners preserved their food and which nutritional benefits it came with. Denmark and southern Sweden is known as Scania were far luckier in terms of growing sustainable food, as it is slightly warmer than Norway and the rest of Sweden, and the soil is considered more fertile.

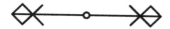

Figure 19 Rye grain, Wikimedia Commons [140]

Rye, see picture above - figure 19 - has been documented in Scandinavia as far back as the Bronze Age; 3.100 BCE to 300 BCE. This nutritious grain was the primary source of sustenance in ancient Scandinavia, as it was not affected much by the harsh winters and heavy rain. Interestingly enough, rye can be grown either in soil or in the sand, such as along the coast on a beach.

The focus back then was sustenance on par or even more prevalent as the taste, so wholegrain rye bread was the norm for Vikings. When it is freezing-level temperatures outside, stuff to be done in the village, boats to build or produce to forage, energy density was paramount. This was why the rye bread baked even back then was the famous variant that you see in the Scandinavian countries today; a thin but incredibly dense, hard-baked, and dark wholegrain rye bread. You will see further down the eye-opening health benefits from this. The Vikings directly thought of this bread as giving them increased vigor and strength. Although they used storytelling, myth-building, and superstition to spread this belief, we today know the actual science behind the truth in that it does indeed provide you more energy and strength. [141]

Scientifically, the type of gluten that the rye grain consists of is different from the more well-known wheat one. Wheat grain's gluten produces a more airy feeling and airy tasting bread when baked. Rye is the opposite, you simply cannot, chemically, get an airy rye bread variant out of the rye grain. [141]

But all about rye you already read about from, "Rye is Fly".

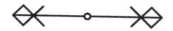

Figure 80 Barley plant, Public Domain

Barley, or 'byg' in Danish, 'korn' in Swedish, and 'bygg' in Norwegian, is another essential cold-weather grain in Scandinavian history, as it was used for bread, flour, beer, and barley porridge. See the picture above for a visual of the barley plant - figure 20. The use of barley in Scandinavia has been documented since the Bronze Age. Barley was also used to feed livestock and cattle since this was highly essential because the animals were also an important food source for survival.

Whole grains have a myriad of nutritional benefits, as we talked about in the "Rye Is Fly" chapter. Most of the grains in the modern world have been heavily modified and processed. But those who eat a diet full of organic and unprocessed grains have a reduced risk of numerous chronic illnesses, and the high fiber tends to ward off obesity and high blood pressure.

Roots such as onions were another favorite among the Nordic people. It was grown underground, which meant it was protected from the volatile weather. Onions were typically planted in early Spring and would be ready within 100 to 150 days.

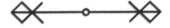

Figure 91 Sea Buckthorn, Wikimedia Commons [142]

Sea Buckthorn

When my wife and I went on a quiet excursion to a secluded summer house area of northern Denmark, we naturally went for frequent walks in nature. By this point, I had known about the wonders and the rather invasive growth of Sea Buckthorn, 'havtorn' in both Danish and Swedish, and 'tindved' in Norwegian. See figure 21 above to get a visual of this bright orange health bomb. See in the northern lands, you can find it in teas, ice cream, alcohol, and jams. The media began with increasing fervency to rave about its properties and the distinct tart taste. When strolling the Danish farmland hills, our feet met the sand. But no brine or salt was smelled. I kneeled down because the plants were still in their infancy. Later, I found out that the Buckthorn can reach anywhere between 7 to 13 feet - 2 to 4 meters in height. And what I saw growing and cultivating was Sea Buckthorn, and I knew that Scandinavia definitely has been taken over by this berry-like invasive plant.

Sea Buckthorn grows close to the sea - why the sea is a part of the name. It has a distinct bright orange look to it and is the size of small grapes.

While this thorn is not strictly Scandinavian, it has become a central part of the Nordic country's food culture. Don't worry we will circle back to this Sea Buckthorn berry later on.

Figure 102 Rosehip, Wikimedia Commons [143]

Rosehip

As a kid in Scandinavia, there is a running, practical joke that you may be subject to.

The joke goes like this: while on the beach, on those few sunny weeks a year up in the Nordic north, you take a fresh rosehip; pry it open; not touching the insides but smear the seeds within on your friend. Then you hoff away and bask from afar the humor on display from your friend being succumbed to a most unstoppable itch accompanied by slurs in one of the three Scandinavian languages.

See, the seeds within the rosehip contain a thin coat of fur: tiny hairs that can give the most awful itch. It is harmless but incredibly hilarious.

To go into the wonders that is the Rosehip; 'hypen' in Danish, 'rosehofte' in Norwegian, and 'nypon' in Swedish, we are neither going into roses nor hips or practical beach jokes. But first, take a look at this itchy and fiery red, poisonous-looking berry in figure 22 above.

We have to go into the world of medicinal products.

Nutritional Benefits

See, in the drying and processing of this bead of red, you remove the hairs and, therefore, the itch. But in its wake, the contents can be used to alleviate joint pains. It can even be used as a natural pain reliever after surgery. It can be used for alleviation from the pains of C-sections. It even shows that it can prevent urinary tract infections after C-section surgery. This lowers the risks of infections in your kidney and bladder in general.

Additionally, Rosehip at face value contains a large amount of fiber, vitamin A, B5, C, and E.

Outside of that, we have the assumed or partially concluded research showing that Rosehip extract is great for skin aging in that it both reduces wrinkles. But also overall skin elasticity. All of this is due to the high value of polyunsaturated fats, which aid your skin's membrane. [144–146]

Likewise, early research indicates that taking Rosehip during a woman's menstrual period alleviates the cramping pains from this.

The list is long, not even mentioning that it can aid sexual problems, bed-wetting, cancer-fighting, and overall immune system strengthening. But as mentioned, more research needs to be conducted here to say for sure. Rosehip is becoming more of popular food, but also rapidly becoming a superfood. [147]

2 pounds - 1 kg - of freshly picked Rosehip
2 cups of water.
400 grams - 14 ounces of cane sugar.
2 fresh, organic lemons.
1 vanilla stick.
1 spoonful of vanilla sugar.
1 spoonful of pectin.

ROSEHIP JAM RECIPE

How to make

Gently peel the Rosehips apart to then empty the seeds within. Once emptied, wash and rinse the two peels left in its wake thoroughly.

Then take your two lemons and wash them as well. Take out your iron and begin to grate or scrape the peel off into a pot.

Add all the Rosehip peels in the bowl, together with some lemon zest, a split vanilla bean, and the remaining juice from the two thoroughly scraped lemons.

BOIL ALL OF THIS, WITH A LID ON, FOR AROUND 20 MINUTES, AND THEN ADD THE SUGAR CANE. CONTINUE BOILING, BUT THIS TIME WITHOUT THE LID, FOR ABOUT 15 MINUTES. THEN ADD THE BOILING JAM TO THE JAR WITH THE LID ON AND PUT IT IN YOUR FRIDGE.

IF YOU WANT IT TO LAST FOR LONGER, ADD ONE TEASPOONFUL OF PECTIN.

Nyponsoppa soup recipe

If the jam is not your thing, first of all, who are you, and what made you just say that? Second of all, the Swedish traditional Rosehip soup of nyponsoppa will be your go-to.

Traditionally in Sweden, which is still being practiced in the Swedish forests today, is the practice of families venturing into the forests to pick fresh Rosehip, to be made into nyponsoppa. This soup is generally used as either a starter, a dessert, or an after-school snack. Historically, nyponsoppa was considered essential for the Swedish folk. Especially, during the latter stages of fall and winter, as this soup was considered crucial for Swedes' health. Because of its many nutritional qualities. When the Swedes were poor, foraging was the method of acquiring food of which the rosehip grew all the way up through long green Sweden, stopping at the arctic circle. [148]

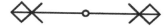

Figure 113 Nyponsoppa, or Rosehip soup, Wikimedia Commons [149]

Serves: 1-2
Prep/Cooking Time: 1 Hour

How to make this soup shown above in figure 23 is to add...

- 3 cups or 400 grams of dried rosehip

- 5 cups of water
- 100 grams or 3.5 ounces of fine sugar
- Optional 0.5 teaspoon vanilla paste
- 2 teaspoons of potato flour

Then to add flavor, you can use either almond flakes, whipped cream, ice cream, or sour cream.

How you go about making nyponsoppa, if you cannot be in a lush Swedish forest during cold wintery darkness...

1. Soak the dried rosehips the night before in 2 cups of water.

2. Then place all the soaked waterlogged rosehip into a bowl and bring it to a boiling point. Let it simmer here for 25 minutes.

3. Then smudge them with an immersion blender or a spoon if you don't have one. Then add the last bit of 3 cups of water.

4. Let it simmer and stew, and allow it to infuse for about 30 minutes.

5. After, use a sieve to filter the loose rosehip, so the liquid is left and placed into a smaller pot. Then add 100 grams or 3.5 ounces of sugar, and then a bit of vanilla paste.

6. At the side mix, blend some flour with some of the liquid to form a loose paste, then take this paste and put it into the soup. Now stir away!

7. Slowly add heat to the soup while you stir continuously until the soup is nice and thick.

8. Now serve and enjoy being a cold Swede in your forest cabin going into the long winter darkness.

History and Culture.

Rosehip was considered the poor man's sustenance in Sweden. This is interesting since over in England, the English botanist lad in 1597 and wrote a book with the succinct title of "The fruit when it is ripe maketh most pleasant meats and banqueting dishes, as tarts and such-like; the making whereof I commit to the cunning cook". If you don't speak fancy old British English, this meant that the aristocracy up until the end of the 16th century in Northern Europe was supplementing their pompous meals with rosehip. [150] Even the medicinal people in the Swedish secluded huts dried rosehip and were documented to be used to treat the plague, worms, and pains. [148]

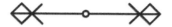

Figure 124 Allotment garden huts in Rodeløkka, Oslo, Norway, Public Domain

Depending on your standard of living in Scandinavia - or your family's proclivity towards nature - you likely have been blessed with having a 'growing garden'. Because many of the typical suburban areas in the North have accompanying small herbal gardens - ironically, growing more than just herbs. Even if you didn't live in curated, sanitary, and bio-controlled plots of land, you would likely own what is known as a kolonihavehus, in Danish, or kolonihage in Norwegian, or tilldelning trädgårdsstuga in Swedish. In internationally friendly English, it would be "allotment garden hut." See figure 24 above to get a traditional visual perspective. These tiny houses would at first glance look like a fancy shed, and at second glance, a shed with a rather nice garden around. By going there to get the glances you would see what endearingly looks like a small village for Norse mythological fauns. Because these allotment huts are littered all around in nature. My family had a garden and a subsequent herbal garden - growing more than herbs - so we had no need for an allotment garden hut.

I distinctly remember, based on the season and how many layers were needed, the Sundays of going to the garden center to buy the seasonal seeds. Most of the time we went in with a plan. Let's grow kale, potatoes, and strawberries. Today is parsley and celery day. But sometimes we just made a trip out of it and let our impulses guide us through the curated greenery made to sell.

Since very young I learned how food was grown and loved: nearly straight rows of seeds turned into less neat lined produce. To then harvest it, move it over to the kitchen, and arrive at its destination at the dinner or lunch table. You learn the importance of clean and organic food. Even the act of life and growing something, making you care that much more about your food.

In short, Scandinavian children raised with an allotment garden hut, communal garden, or an owned herbal garden, learn the importance of the aesthetics of the everyday. How the science and our cultivation practices of growing can grow the appreciation of what is growing. But also the passage of seasons and how our human temporal range - time perception - can change based on adopting the lifecycle of that strawberry plant or that beetroot or those potato knots. It led, at least in my case, to a universal sense of appreciation of natural environments and land. A valuable lesson indeed.

Nutritional Benefits.

Food grown from the soil offers a variety of nutritional benefits, mainly because it is completely organic and natural. Root and bulb vegetables contain all of the delicious benefits that we need for our health; including fiber, potassium, and Vitamin C, to name a few. These rich roots tend to be low in fat and carbohydrates as well, making them a perfect healthy snack or dinner addition.

Sweet potatoes have more antioxidants than white potatoes. Although, white potatoes contain more fiber and calories, which was important in case there was ever a food shortage.

Beetroots are notorious for their bright red/purple color, and distinct "earthy" or "dirt" taste. The red pigment in beetroot is linked with its high iron content. Since before year 0, beetroot was used medicinally before it was eaten, grown wildly at some beaches in Europe, and also found in Denmark. 10 to 14 percent of people can't digest this bright red vegetable, which results in your urine becoming purple-ish red, a harmless yet alarming occurrence. What gives it the earthy and dirt taste is geosmin, a harmless taste that can actually be removed if preferred. Historically, fried beetroot was used as a coffee replacement when coffee beans were not available or too expensive.

Berries are known for their bright colors and sweet taste, but these are sugary treats that you won't feel guilty about. In fact, berries help to control blood sugar, whereas traditional sweet treats will raise it. Ancient Scandinavians grazed on these berries as a source of energy and nutrition as they were so easily accessible.

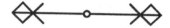

Figure 135 Bilberry, or blueberry, Wikimedia Commons [151]

The bilberry is a Nordic berry closely related to the blueberry in appearance and size. In fact, it is even called the same in English. Which makes sense, if you take a look at the picture, figure 25 above. So much so that the translation of the berry is the same as the blueberry in the various Scandinavian languages: "blåbær" in Danish and Norwegian, and "blåbär" in Swedish. The bilberry grows freely in Scandinavia and is often confused for blueberries. However, they are slightly darker and smaller than the typical blueberry. The only real difference in these blue superfoods is the taste, as bilberries are juicier and sweeter. Bilberries are packed full of antioxidants, and in the name itself, this compound protects you from oxidative stress in your body. The benefits of this little berry even extend to your vision, brain, and heart. It's no wonder why the ancient Vikings were so large and strong!

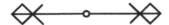

Figure 146 Lingonberries in Sweden, Public Domain

"Tyttebær" in Danish and the small variant of "tytebær" in Norwegian, or the more international "lingon" in Swedish. All of these names refer to the lingonberry, for those who aren't fluent in one of the Scandinavian languages. See the small but hard-hitting berry above in figure 26. And is another juicy little treat that many Scandinavians are familiar with.

The name "lingonberry" comes from the Swedish word "lingon," and this word is of course derived from the old Norse word "lyngr," which means heather. [152] Lingonberries are found all throughout Scandinavia and even Finland, and they are very similar to cranberries in appearance and taste. A study on this particular berry was conducted at the University of Helsinki in Finland, to determine the actual benefits of this Nordic berry. In a study conducted on ill rats, it was found that the lingonberry has profound effects on...

It's no wonder that this tiny fruit is one of Finland's most popular berries. To receive the full benefit of the Lingonberry, this fruit is best eaten raw or juiced, rather than cooked or boiled.

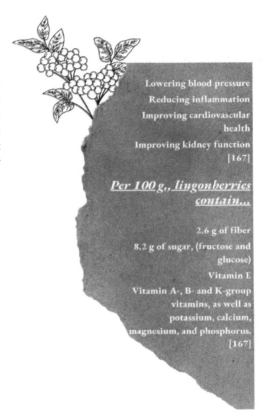

Lowering blood pressure
Reducing inflammation
Improving cardiovascular health
Improving kidney function
[167]

Per 100 g., lingonberries contain...

2.6 g of fiber
8.2 g of sugar, (fructose and glucose)
Vitamin E
Vitamin A-, B- and K-group vitamins, as well as potassium, calcium, magnesium, and phosphorus.
[167]

The Incredible Sea Buckthorn.

One Sea Buckthorn grape, (fly up to figure 21 to get a reminder of how the Sea Buckthorn looks like) contains as much C-vitamin as a whole orange. A grape that is smaller in size than a wine grape at that.

It is stock-full of Vitamin E, carotenoids, flavonoids, and plenty of fatty acids and vitamin B1, B2, B6, and B12. There is even the less common vitamin E and K, polyphenols, fiber, amino acids, and minerals such as potassium, manganese, iron, and copper. To add to the mix, the grapes also contain healthy amounts of folate and biotin. All these reasons make the Sea Buckthorn grape a superfood.

When we begin to cold press, extracting the oils from the seeds with the Sea Buckthorn, we start to get omega fatty acids vital to our health - some naturally found in fish. The ones being omega-3, omega-6, omega-7, and omega-9. [153] Incredible!

All around the world Sea Buckthorn has been used for medicinal purposes. But specifically, Russia and China adopted the Buckthorn into their healing properties and salves. In some ways, it is interesting to write about this wonder mini-grape here in this Scandinavian diet book, since one of its well-known nicknames is "the Holy Fruit of the Himalayas". To go into the specifics of the Sea Buckthorn benefits the list will get lengthy. Although, due to the new discoveries and the cultural rave all about this thorn, the studies of this grape are new and usually only animal-based.

Sea Buckthorn is said to remove what is known as "free radicals". Free radicals are essentially molecules that go in and damage cells in your body. Other excellent Sea Buckthorn benefits are... [154]

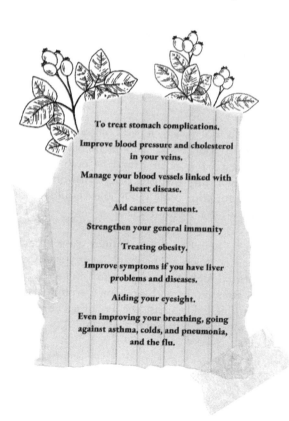

To treat stomach complications.

Improve blood pressure and cholesterol in your veins.

Manage your blood vessels linked with heart disease.

Aid cancer treatment.

Strengthen your general immunity

Treating obesity.

Improve symptoms if you have liver problems and diseases.

Aiding your eyesight.

Even improving your breathing, going against asthma, colds, and pneumonia, and the flu.

In some other instances, people have been known to use Sea Buckthorn as an ointment for sunburned skin. Fighting against radiation damage, skin rashes, general burns, and improving acne.

Sea Buckthorn is particularly good for **heart health**. Heart disease in many countries is the number 1 killer of its citizens. See the antioxidants contained within are likely to fight against blood clots, blood pressure, and cholesterol levels. Essentially, if you are prone to having a heart condition or having higher blood pressure than normal or high cholesterol, then Sea Buckthorn is absolutely your friend. [155]

The other condition to shine a spotlight on is **diabetes**; whether it be from diet or from your genetics. Evidence shows that Sea Buckthorn counteracts, or at least fights off diabetes. It has been proven that Type 2 Diabetes can be managed by a healthy diet and adequate exercise alone. [156]

It was found that applying Sea Buckthorn oil to wounds and sunburns can help your skin regenerate and heal quicker and fuller. [157] This was even the case with a Placebo-controlled test which found that applying Sea Buckthorn mixed with water created tighter and **healthier skin** elasticity. [158]

Lastly, but definitely not least, it was shown that Sea Buckthorn can **fight cancer cells** in your body. This element comes from the high content of quercetin which has been found to help fight cancer cells in general. [159] It even was found that Sea Buckthorn oil can prevent cancer from spreading throughout your body [160], and should be a staple in your diet if ever diagnosed with that awful disease.

And with all these benefits, very limited side effects have been documented. In rare cases, people who have been treated with high doses of Sea Buckthorn reported higher blood pressure, headaches, and dizziness. While it is known to thin out your blood, in extreme cases, it can cause bleeding. But as mentioned, like with the benefits, empirical evidence is limited and mostly connected with animal testing. Try it out for yourself and see how you feel!

In conclusion, we would like to thank all readers and listeners for embarking on this culinary journey with us and hope you have been enlightened and educated in the way that was intended. We hope you will use this not only as a one-time reading. But as a reference for later use. Whether it be to recite interesting facts or even try out one of the famous Nordic recipes.

If we also could humbly ask you to leave a review of your thoughts on this book. This has been a project that our small family has been occupied with for a while, and hope that you liked it!

And again if you whiz all the way to the top you will find all of our books. Just write an email, sign up, and you will get any of these books for free.

Thank

you.

SOURCES AND ACKNOWLEDGEMENTS

[1]   Nielsen AHH, Dyekjær MS, Bjørn J. Tv-værter ser tilbage: Sådan blev 'Score-Kaj', 'Hr. Skæg' og 'Gæt en lort' født. Danmarks Radio 2018. https://www.dr.dk/nyheder/kultur/film/tv-vaerter-ser-tilbage-saadan-blev-score-kaj-hr-skaeg-og-gaet-en-lort-foedt.

[2]   World Health Organization - Europe. Spotlight on adolescent health and well-being: Health Behaviour in School-aged Children (HBSC) survey in Europe and Canada. 2018.

[3]   Hill A. What Is Mead, and Is It Good for You? Healthline 2018. https://www.healthline.com/nutrition/mead#benefits.

[4]   LEWANDOWSKI P. MEAD AND THE VIKINGS. War Rocks 2016. https://warontherocks.com/2016/01/mead-and-the-vikings/.

[5]   Batch Mead. Vikings + Mead = ? What is Viking Mead. BatchmeadCom 2020. https://www.batchmead.com/blog/vikings-mead.

[6]   The Editors of Encyclopaedia Britannica. Mead. Britannica 2021. https://www.britannica.com/topic/mead.

[7]   Meo SA, Al-Asiri SA, Mahesar AL, Ansarid MJ. Role of honey in modern medicine. Saudi J Biol Sci 2017;24:975–8.

[8]   Nazir Y, Hussain SA, Hamid AA, Song Y. Probiotics and Their Potential Preventive and Therapeutic Role for Cancer, High Serum Cholesterol, and Allergic and HIV Diseases. Biomed Res Int 2018.

[9]   Varankovich N V., Nickerson MT, Korber DR. Probiotic-based strategies for therapeutic and prophylactic use against multiple gastrointestinal diseases. Front Microbiol 2015;6:685.

[10]   Engen PA, Green SJ, Voigt RM, Forsyth CB, Keshavarzian A. The Gastrointestinal Microbiome. Alcohol Res Curr Rev 2015;37:223–236.

[11]   Spicers of Hythe. A HISTORY OF MULLED WINE. Spicers of
         Hythe 2016. https://www.spicersofhythe.co.uk/a-history-of-
         mulled-wine/#.

[12]   Grynkiewicz G, Demchuk OM. New Perspectives for Fisetin. Front
         Chem 2019;7:697.

[13]   Sarubbo F, Esteban S, Miralles A, Moranta D. Effects of
         Resveratrol and other Polyphenols on Sirt1: Relevance to Brain
         Function During Aging. Curr Neuropharmacol 2018;16:126–136.

[14]   Lee S-H, Lee J-H, Lee H-Y, Min K-J. Sirtuin signaling in cellular
         senescence and aging. BMB Reports Online 2019;52:24–34.

[15]   Benslimane Y, Bertomeu T, Coulombe-Huntington J, McQuaid M,
         Sánchez-Osuna M, Papadopoli D, et al. Genome-Wide Screens
         Reveal that Resveratrol Induces Replicative Stress in Human Cells.
         Mol Cell 2020;79:846–56.

[16]   Poulose SM, Thangthaeng N, Miller MG, Shukitt-Hale B. Effects of
         pterostilbene and resveratrol on brain and behavior. Neurochem Int
         2015:227–33.

[17]   Leech J. 9 Evidence-Based Health Benefits of Almonds. Healthline
         2018. https://www.healthline.com/nutrition/9-proven-benefits-of-
         almonds#TOC_TITLE_HDR_3.

[18]   Rietschier HL, Henagan TM, Earnest CP, Baker BL, Cortez CC,
         Stewart LK. Sun-dried raisins are a cost-effective alternative to
         Sports Jelly Beans in prolonged cycling. J Strength Cond Res
         2011;11:3150–6.

[19]   Smylique. Beyond a Pretty Smile: 9 Surprising Health Benefits of
         Good Oral Hygiene. SmyliqueCom 2021.
         https://www.smylique.com/blog/beyond-a-pretty-smile-9-
         surprising-health-benefits-of-good-oral-hygiene.

[20]   Wu CD. Grape Products and Oral Health. J Nutr 2009;139:1818–
         1823.

[21]   Qiblawi S, Al-Hazimi A, Al-Mogbel M, Hossain A, Bagchi D.
         Chemopreventive effects of cardamom (Elettaria cardamomum L.)
         on chemically induced skin carcinogenesis in Swiss albino mice. J
         Med Food 2012;6:576–80.

[22]   Das I, Acharya A, Berry DL, Sen S, Williams E, Permaul E, et al.
         Antioxidative effects of the spice cardamom against non-melanoma
         skin cancer by modulating nuclear factor erythroid-2-related factor 2
         and NF-ĸB signalling pathways. Br J Nutr 2012;108:984–97.

[23]   Majdalawieh AF, Carr RI. In vitro investigation of the potential
         immunomodulatory and anti-cancer activities of black pepper (Piper
         nigrum) and cardamom (Elettaria cardamomum). J Med Food
         2010;2:371–81.

[24]   Jou Y-J, Chen C-J, Liu Y-C, Way T-D, La C-H, Hua C-H, et al.

Quantitative phosphoproteomic analysis reveals γ-bisabolene inducing p53-mediated apoptosis of human oral squamous cell carcinoma via HDAC2 inhibition and ERK1/2 activation. Proteomics 2015;19:3296–309.

[25]   Jamal A, Javed K, Aslam M, Jafri MA. Gastroprotective effect of cardamom, Elettaria cardamomum Maton. fruits in rats. J Ethnopharmacol 2006;103:149–53.

[26]   Patil S, Sreekumaran E, Krishna AP. EVALUATION OF THE EFFICACY OF CARDAMOM AROMATHERAPY ON AEROBIC FITNESS & AUTONOMIC FUNCTIONS AMONG STUDENTS. 1 2 1. J Heal Allied Sci NU 2011.

[27]   Lim D-W, Kim H, Park J-Y, Kim J-E, Moon J-Y, Park S-D, et al. Amomum cardamomum L. ethyl acetate fraction protects against carbon tetrachloride-induced liver injury via an antioxidant mechanism in rats. BMC Complmentary Altern Med 2016;16:155.

[28]   Ali S, Prasad R, Mahmood A, Routray I, Shinkafi TS, Sahin K, et al. Eugenol-rich Fraction of Syzygium aromaticum (Clove) Reverses Biochemical and Histopathological Changes in Liver Cirrhosis and Inhibits Hepatic Cell Proliferation. J Cancer Prev 2014;19:288–300.

[29]   Kuroda M, Mimaki Y, Ohtomo T, Yamada J, Nishiyama T, Mae T, et al. Hypoglycemic effects of clove (Syzygium aromaticum flower buds) on genetically diabetic KK-Ay mice and identification of the active ingredients. J Nat Med 2012;2:394–9.

[30]   Anh NH, Kim SJ, Long NP, Min JE, Yoon YC, Lee EG, et al. Ginger on Human Health: A Comprehensive Systematic Review of 109 Randomized Controlled Trials. Nutrients 2020;12:157.

[31]   Soltani E, Jangjoo A, Aghaei MA, Dalili A. Effects of preoperative administration of ginger (Zingiber officinale Roscoe) on postoperative nausea and vomiting after laparoscopic cholecystectomy. J Tradit Complement Med 2018;8:387–390.

[32]   Crichton M, Marshall S, Marx W, McCarthy AL, Isenring E. Efficacy of Ginger (Zingiber officinale) in Ameliorating Chemotherapy-Induced Nausea and Vomiting and Chemotherapy-Related Outcomes: A Systematic Review Update and Meta-Analysis. J Acad Nutr Diet 2019;119:2055–68.

[33]   Bartels EM, Folmer VN, Bliddal H, Altman RD, Juhl C, Tarp S, et al. Efficacy and safety of ginger in osteoarthritis patients: a meta-analysis of randomized placebo-controlled trials. Osteoarthr Cartil 2015;23:13–21.

[34]   Ozgoli G, Goli M, Moattar F. Comparison of effects of ginger, mefenamic acid, and ibuprofen on pain in women with primary dysmenorrhea. J Altern Complement Med 2009;15:129–32.

[35]   Chen CX, Barrett B, Kwekkeboom KL. Efficacy of Oral Ginger

(Zingiber officinale) for Dysmenorrhea: A Systematic Review and Meta-Analysis. Evid Based Complement Altern Med 2016.

[36]   Sommer MP. Hvorfor elsker nisser risengrød? VidenskabDk 2015. https://videnskab.dk/sporg-videnskaben/hvorfor-elsker-nisser-risengrod.

[37]   Tingstrøm MB. 1800-tallets borgerskab skabte julenissen. VidenskabDk 2009. https://videnskab.dk/kultur-samfund/1800-tallets-borgerskab-skabte-julenissen.

[38]   LALASZ B. Nature Makes Us Smarter. OK, Now What? Cool Green Sci 2015. https://blog.nature.org/science/2015/06/05/nature-smarter-cognitive/.

[39]   SUTTIE J. How Nature Can Make You Kinder, Happier, and More Creative. Gt Good Mag - Sci Insights a Meaningful Life 2016. https://greatergood.berkeley.edu/article/item/how_nature_makes_you_kinder_happier_more_creative/.

[40]   Health Benefits Times. Chanterelle mushroom – Cantharellus californicus. Heal Benefits Times 2021. https://www.healthbenefitstimes.com/chanterelle-mushroom/.

[41]   Thole JM, Kraft TFB, Sueiro LA, Kang Y-H, Gills JJ, Cuendet M, et al. A comparative evaluation of the anticancer properties of European and American elderberry fruits. J Med Food 2006;9:498–504.

[42]   Porter RS, Bode RF. A Review of the Antiviral Properties of Black Elder (Sambucus nigra L.) Products. Phyther Res 2017;31:533–54.

[43]   Sidor A, Gramza-Michałowska A. Advanced research on the antioxidant and health benefit of elderberry (Sambucus nigra) in food – a review. J Funct Foods 2015;18:941–58.

[44]   Mandl E, Richter A. Elderberry: Benefits and Dangers. Healthline 2021. https://www.healthline.com/nutrition/elderberry.

[45]   mydanishkitchen. My Danish Kitchen. MydanishkitchenCom 2012. https://mydanishkitchen.com/2012/06/04/hyldeblomst-saft-elderflower-drink/.

[46]   Barker J. The Medicinal Flora of Britain and Northwestern Europe. 2001.

[47]   Grieve M, Leyel CF, Leyel MCF. A Modern Herbal. 1996.

[48]   Nodal JH, Milner G. "A" Glossary of the Lancashire Dialect: F to Z. 1882.

[49]   Thiem B. Rubus chamaemorus L. - a boreal plant rich in biologically active metabolites: A review. Pozn Univ Med Sci 2003.

[50]   Villalba KJO, Barka FV, Pasos CV, Rodríguez PE. Food Ellagitannins: Structure, Metabolomic Fate, and Biological Properties. 2019.

[51] Culpeper N. THE ENGLISH PHYSICIAN MEDICINES MADE OF ENGLISH HERBS. 1663.

[52] Cobb C, Chertoff J. What Is Astringent? Healthline 2019. https://www.healthline.com/health/beauty-skin-care/astringent#benefits.

[53] Chin K, McDermott A. Blackberries: Health Benefits and Nutrition Information. Healthline1 2021. https://www.healthline.com/health/benefits-of-blackberries.

[54] Miller MG, Shukitt-Hale B. Berry Fruit Enhances Beneficial Signaling in the Brain. J Agric Food Chem 2012;60:5709–5715.

[55] González OA, Escamilla C, Danaher RJ, Dai J, Ebersole JL, Mumper RJ, et al. Antibacterial Effects of Blackberry Extract Target Periodontopathogens. J Periodontal Res 2014;48:80–6.

[56] Dental Innovations. THE BENEFITS OF GOOD ORAL HYGIENE. DentalinnCom 2021. https://dentalinn.com/oral-hygiene-benefits-lincoln-square/.

[57] Meixner M. Electrolyte Water: Benefits and Myths. Healthline 2018. https://www.healthline.com/nutrition/electrolyte-water.

[58] McGrane K, Bjarnadottir A. What Is Birch Water? Benefits and Downsides. Healthline 2019. https://www.healthline.com/nutrition/birch-sap#bottom-line.

[59] Blount M. Folklore of The Silver Birch n.d.:3.

[60] Wikipedia. Smoking (cooking) - History. Wikipedia 2021. https://en.wikipedia.org/wiki/Smoking_(cooking)#History.

[61] Venema C. Smoking as a food cooking method. Michigan State Univ Ext 2016. https://www.canr.msu.edu/news/smoking_as_a_food_cooking_method.

[62] chadsbbq. The History of Smoked Meat. Chadsbbq 2017. https://www.chadsbbq.com/the-history-of-smoked-meat/.

[63] madfeed. The MAD Guide to Smoking Foods. MadfeedCo 2015. https://madfeed.co/2015/the-madfeed-guide-to-smoking-foods/.

[64] louisiana-grills. 7 PREMIUM BENEFITS OF SMOKING MEAT. Louisiana-GrillsCom 2021. https://louisiana-grills.com/beyond-the-grill/7-premium-benefits-of-smoking-meat.

[65] Ribe VikingeCenter. Smoking fish and meat - Preservation and flavour. Ribe VikingeCenter Nord Food Is Viking Food - Reg Syddanmark 2012. https://www.ribevikingecenter.dk/en/learn-more/food/food-smoking.aspx.

[66] Qoura Experts. How did the Vikings preserve their meat? Qoura 2019. https://www.quora.com/How-did-the-Vikings-preserve-their-meat.

[67] Brown D. Propane smoker. Wikimedia Commons 2008.

https://en.wikipedia.org/wiki/File:Propane_smoker.jpg.

[68]   Grillmastersclub. ULTIMATE BEGINNERS GUIDE ON HOW
        TO SMOKE MEAT AT HOME LIKE A PRO.
        GrillmastersclubCom 2020. https://grillmastersclub.com/ultimate-
        beginners-guide-smoke-meat-home-like-pro/.

[69]   Grumpy Lokean Elder. Question: What sweets did the vikings eat?
        Tumblr 2013.
        https://grumpylokeanelder.tumblr.com/post/56087979418/questio
        n-what-sweets-did-the-vikings-eat.

[70]   Dutta M. Why Scandinavia is the most underrated destination for
        pastry lovers. Matador Netw 2018.
        https://matadornetwork.com/read/scandinavia-underrated-
        destination-pastry-lovers/.

[71]   ASANATH. USES AND MEDICINAL PROPERTIES OF
        CINNAMON. Wild Tumeric 2021. https://www.wild-
        turmeric.com/2021/03/uses-and-medicinal-properties-of.html.

[72]   Axelsson M. Varför är kanelbullens dag den 4 oktober? Högtider
        Och Tradit 2009.
        https://svenskahogtider.com/2009/10/03/varfor-ar-kanelbullens-
        dag-den-4-oktober/.

[73]   Shan B, Cai YZ, Sun M, Corke H. Antioxidant capacity of 26 spice
        extracts and characterization of their phenolic constituents. J Agric
        Food Chem 2005;53:7749–59.

[74]   Mancini-Filho J, Van-Koiij A, Mancini DA, Cozzolino FF, Torres
        RP. Antioxidant activity of cinnamon (Cinnamomum Zeylanicum,
        Breyne) extracts. Boll Chim Farm 1998;137:443–7.

[75]   Adisakwattana S, Lerdsuwankij O, Poputtachai U, Minipun A,
        Suparpprom C. Inhibitory activity of cinnamon bark species and
        their combination effect with acarbose against intestinal α-
        glucosidase and pancreatic α-amylase. Plant Foods Hum Nutr
        2011;66:143–8.

[76]   Shihabudeen HMS, Priscilla DH, Thirumurugan K. Cinnamon
        extract inhibits α-glucosidase activity and dampens postprandial
        glucose excursion in diabetic rats. Nutr Metab London 2011;8:46.

[77]   WebMD - Diet & Weight Management. Cinnamon. WebMD 2021.
        https://www.webmd.com/diet/supplement-guide-cinnamon#1.

[78]   Rao PV, Gan SH. Cinnamon: A Multifaceted Medicinal Plant.
        Evidence-Based Complement Altern Med 2014.

[79]   Dhuley JN. Anti-oxidant effects of cinnamon (Cinnamomum
        verum) bark and greater cardamom (Amomum subulatum) seeds in
        rats fed high fat diet. Indian J Exp Biol 1999;37:238–42.

[80]   Kumar S, Vasudeva N, Sharma S. GC-MS analysis and screening of
        antidiabetic, antioxidant and hypolipidemic potential of

Cinnamomum tamala oil in streptozotocin induced diabetes mellitus in rats. Cardiovasc Diabetol 2012;11:95.

[81] Qin B, Panickar KS, Anderson RA. Cinnamon: Potential Role in the Prevention of Insulin Resistance, Metabolic Syndrome, and Type 2 Diabetes. J Diabetes Sci Technol From Basic Sci to Clin Pract 2010;4:685–693.

[82] Anderson RA. Chromium and polyphenols from cinnamon improve insulin sensitivity. Proc Nutr Soc 2008;67:48–53.

[83] Bhattacharjee S, Rana T, Sengupta A. Inhibition of lipid peroxidation and enhancement of GST activity by cardamom and cinnamon during chemically induced colon carcinogenesis in Swiss albino mice. Asian Pacific J Cancer Prev 2007;8:578–82.

[84] Singh HB, Srivastava M, Singh AB, Srivastava AK. Cinnamon bark oil, a potent fungitoxicant against fungi causing respiratory tract mycoses. Allergy 1995;50:995–9.

[85] Ooi LSM, Li Y, Kam S-L, Wang H, Wong EYL, Ooi VEC. Antimicrobial activities of cinnamon oil and cinnamaldehyde from the Chinese medicinal herb Cinnamomum cassia Blume. Am J Chin Med 2006;34:511–22.

[86] Premanathan M, Rajendran S, Ramanathan T, Kathiresan K, Nakashima H, Yamamoto N. A survey of some Indian medicinal plants for anti-human immunodeficiency virus (HIV) activity. Indian J Med Res 2000;112:73–7.

[87] N/A. Spandauer. Biblioteksvagten 2012. https://www.biblioteksvagten.dk/tidligere-svar.php?quid=150024-bibvagt:aeaf49c0-20bb-08a4-6d10-e7329999988f.

[88] Wikipedia. Danish pastry. Wikipedia 2021. https://en.wikipedia.org/wiki/Danish_pastry.

[89] cyclonebill. File:Fastelavnsboller (6911368341).jpg. Wikimedia Commons 2012. https://commons.wikimedia.org/wiki/File:Fastelavnsboller_(69113 68341).jpg.

[90] Sørensen AM. De originale fastelavnsbolle-opskrifter: Du må først spise dem på tirsdag! VidenskabDk 2018. https://videnskab.dk/kultur-samfund/de-originale-fastelavnsbolle-opskrifter-du-maa-foerst-spise-dem-paa-tirsdag.

[91] SØRENSEN AG. 8 ting du (måske) ikke vidste om fastelavnsboller. SamvirkeDk 2014. https://samvirke.dk/artikler/8-ting-du-maaske-ikke-vidste-om-fastelavnsboller.

[92] Rosendahl S, Møller G. Det vidste du ikke om koldskål. CoopDk - Opskrifter 2018. https://opskrifter.coop.dk/artikler/det-vidste-du-ikke-om-koldskaal.

[93] Wojcik J. Hvorfor hedder det kammerjunkere? VidenskabDk 2012.

https://videnskab.dk/sporg-videnskaben/hvorfor-hedder-det-kammerjunkere.

[94]   Skandi Baking. Rødgrød Med Fløde (Berry Porridge with Cream). Skandi Bak 2021. https://skandibaking.com/rodgrod-med-flode-berry-porridge-with-cream/?utm_source=rss&utm_medium=rss&utm_campaign=rodgrod-med-flode-berry-porridge-with-cream.

[95]   Nielsen K. DANISH COLD BUTTERMILK SOUP (KOLDSKÅL). Nord Food Living 2021. https://nordicfoodliving.com/danish-cold-buttermilk-soup-koldskal/.

[96]   Havard Health Publishing. Why nutritionists are crazy about nuts. Havard Heal Publ 2017. https://www.health.harvard.edu/nutrition/why-nutritionists-are-crazy-about-nuts.

[97]   Gunnars K. 10 Surprising Health Benefits of Honey. Healthline 2018. https://www.healthline.com/nutrition/10-benefits-of-honey#TOC_TITLE_HDR_5.

[98]   MyPlate - U.S. Department of Agriculture. Dairy. MyPlate - US Dep Agric 2020. https://www.myplate.gov/eat-healthy/dairy.

[99]   SUCCESSB440. Norwegian Krumkake. All Recipes 2007. https://www.allrecipes.com/recipe/68293/norwegian-krumkake/.

[100]   Studentchef. HONEY NUT CAKE. FoodCom 2010. https://www.food.com/recipe/honey-nut-cake-428008.

[101]   MILES-MEREDITHTHOMPSON. Praline Ice Cream Dessert. Yummly 2017. https://www.yummly.com/recipe/Praline-Ice-Cream-Dessert-1386311#1184abca-848d-4f83-877c-f8fd19da72de.

[102]   Perabo L. How would Viking Age Scandinavian fishermen have worked? Quora 2017. https://www.quora.com/How-would-Viking-Age-Scandinavian-fishermen-have-worked.

[103]   Todd N. Omega-3 Fish Oil Supplements for Heart Disease. WebMDb 2021. https://www.webmd.com/hypertension-high-blood-pressure/guide/omega-3-fish-oil-supplements-for-high-blood-pressure#:~:text=Omega%252D3%2520fish%2520oil%2520contains,Lower%2520blood%25 20pressure.

[104]   The Editors of Encyclopaedia Britannica. Ecological and commercial importance. Britannica 2021. https://www.britannica.com/science/algae/Ecological-and-commercial-importance.

[105]   Arnarson A, Buettner K. Kelp Benefits: A Health Booster from the Sea. Healthline 2020. healthline.com/health/food-nutrition/benefits-of-kelp#nutrition.

[106]   Roberts K, Talebian S. Kelp: The Oceanic Plant With Skin, Health
         & Thyroid Benefits*. Mindbodygreen 2020.
         https://www.mindbodygreen.com/articles/kelp-the-health-
         benefits-and-supplements.

[107]   History Hit. Why Did the Vikings Invade Britain? Hist Hit 2019.
         https://www.historyhit.com/why-did-the-vikings-invade-
         britain/#:~:text=Anglo-Saxon E ngland was very,own commerce
         with the region.

[108]   Wikipedia. Viking Age. Wikipedia 2021.
         https://en.wikipedia.org/wiki/Viking_Age#:~:text=The Viking
         Age (793–1 066,and the Germanic Iron Age.

[109]   Whatscookingamerica. Lutefisk History and Recipe.
         Whatscookingamerica 2016.
         https://whatscookingamerica.net/History/LutefiskHistory.htm.

[110]   Wikipedia. Lutefisk. Wikipedia 2021.
         https://en.wikipedia.org/wiki/Lutefisk#:~:text=It%2520is%2520
         made%2520from%2520aged,dish%2520of%25
         20several%2520Nordic%2520countries.

[111]   Norwegianamerican. "The Great Lutefisk Mystery," solved.
         Norwegianamerican 2021.
         https://www.norwegianamerican.com/the-great-lutefisk-mystery-
         solved/.

[112]   Duxbury J. Prawns on Toast. SwedishFood 2021.
         https://www.swedishfood.com/swedish-food-recipes-starters/109-
         prawns-on-toast.

[113]   Mark JJ. Norse-Viking Diet. World Hist Organ 2019.
         https://www.worldhistory.org/article/1311/norse-viking-diet/.

[114]   BUTLER S. The Surprisingly Sufficient Viking Diet. HistoryCom
         2019. https://www.history.com/news/the-surprisingly-sufficient-
         viking-diet.

[115]   N/A. When a chicken (or any meat) is boiled, what nutritional value
         is lost if only the meat is consumed, and not the broth? (This is for
         my cat to eat). Quora 2020. https://www.quora.com/When-a-
         chicken-or-any-meat-is-boiled-what-nutritional-value-is-lost-if-only-
         the-meat-is-consumed-and-not-the-broth-This-is-for-my-cat-to-eat.

[116]   AHDB. Six reasons why beef is good for you. AHDB 2021.
         https://ahdb.org.uk/red-meat-and-health-beef.

[117]   Duxbury J. Pork with apple Äppelfläsk. SwedishFood 2021.
         https://www.swedishfood.com/swedish-food-recipes-main-
         courses/224-pork-with-apple.

[118]   Harada S, Furukawa M, Tokuoka E, Matsumoto K, Yahiro S,
         Miyasaka J, et al. [Control of toxicity of Sarcocystis fayeri in
         horsemeat by freezing treatment and prevention of food poisoning

caused by raw consumption of horsemeat]. Food Hyg Saf Sci 2013;54:198–203.

[119] Kumar A. What are the benefits of eating horse meat? Quora 2019. https://www.quora.com/What-are-the-benefits-of-eating-horse-meat.

[120] Kjørstad E. Here's how Vikings celebrated Christmas. Sciencenorway 2020. https://sciencenorway.no/christmas-history-literature/heres-how-vikings-celebrated-christmas/1788632.

[121] Roswell T. Riding To The Afterlife: The Role Of Horses In Early Medieval North-Western Europe. 2012.

[122] Survive the Jive. Pagan Origin of Horse Meat Taboo. YouTube 2013.

[123] Eggleston B. Decision theory. Cambridge Hist. Moral Philos., 2017. https://doi.org/10.1017/9781139519267.054.

[124] Diamond J. Guns, Germs, and Steel: The Fates of Human Societies. 20th Anniv. W. W. Norton & Company; 2017.

[125] Lyonbakery. The Origin of Bread. LyonbakeryCom 2017. http://lyonbakery.com/the-origin-of-bread/#:~:text=According to history%2C the earliest,) or tortillas (Mexico).

[126] Laughing Historically. BREAD: The History | Laughing Historically. YouTube 2020. https://www.youtube.com/watch?v=oOjc4KZTWzg.

[127] Wikipedia. History of bread. Wikipedia 2021. https://en.wikipedia.org/wiki/History_of_bread.

[128] StoneAgeMan. The History of Bread - The Chemistry of Baking Soda and Yeast. YouTube 2013. https://www.youtube.com/watch?v=qylxpwNhFYI.

[129] Farah T. Banned bread: why does the US allow additives that Europe says are unsafe? Guard 2019. https://www.theguardian.com/us-news/2019/may/28/bread-additives-chemicals-us-toxic-america.

[130] Wasa. About Us - We Are Wasa. WasaCom 2021. https://www.wasa.com/global/about-us/.

[131] GUILFOYLE A. WHAT'S UP WITH RYE? AND WHY DO SWEDES LOVE IT? Umgåsmagazine 2021. http://www.umgasmagazine.com/whats-up-with-rye-and-why-do-swedes-love-it/#:~:text=%25E2%2580%259CIn%2520most%2520parts%2520of%2520Sweden,of%2520fiber%252C%2520than%2520wheat.%25E2%2580%259%2520D.

[132] Estrada J. Is Rye Bread Actually Good for You? A Doctor and RD Weigh In. Well + Good - Food Nutr 2019. https://www.wellandgood.com/is-rye-bread-good-for-you/.

[133]   Rye and Health. Rye Bread. Rye Heal 2014.
        https://www.sciencedirect.com/topics/agricultural-and-biological-
        sciences/rye-bread.
[134]   Raman R, Kubala J. Is Rye Bread Healthy? Healthline 2019.
        https://www.healthline.com/nutrition/is-rye-bread-
        healthy#nutrition.
[135]   Arctic Grub: Culture & History Food. Trilogy of Scandinavian
        Breads Part 1. Arct Grub Cult Hist Food 2013.
        https://arcticgrub.com/trilogy-of-scandinavian-breads-part-1-rye-
        bread/#:~:text=The viking s were the first,most often used in
        Norway.
[136]   Wikipedia. Vikings. Wikipedia 2021.
        https://en.wikipedia.org/wiki/Vikings.
[137]   Fotevikensmuseum.se. Baking bread during the Viking Age:
        Ölandish frying pan bread. Fotevikensmuseum 2021.
        https://www.fotevikensmuseum.se/d/en/vikingar/hur/mat/recept
        /brod.
[138]   NEVADA. Viking Plankefisk and Rugbrød (Plank Fish and Rye
        Bread). Northwildkitchen 2016.
        https://northwildkitchen.com/viking-plankefisk/.
[139]   BAUER E. Homemade Rye Bread. Simplyrecipes 2021.
        https://www.simplyrecipes.com/recipes/georges_light_rye_bread/.
[140]   LSDSL. Ear of rye. Wikimedia Commons 2007.
        https://commons.wikimedia.org/wiki/File:Ear_of_rye.jpg.
[141]   Arctic Grub: Culture & History Food. Trilogy of Scandinavian
        Breads Part 1 Rye Bread. Arct Grub 2013.
        https://arcticgrub.com/trilogy-of-scandinavian-breads-part-1-rye-
        bread/.
[142]   Bgelo777. Ripe berries of sea-buckthorn. Wikimedia Commons
        2018.
        https://commons.wikimedia.org/wiki/File:Ripe_berries_of_sea-
        buckthorn._Selenginsky_district,_Buryatia,_Russia.jpg.
[143]   Morn the Gorn. Rose hips. Wikimedia Commons 2006.
        https://commons.wikimedia.org/wiki/File:Rose_hips.jpg.
[144]   Lei Z, Cao Z, Yang Z, Ao M, Jin W, Yu L. Rosehip Oil Promotes
        Excisional Wound Healing by Accelerating the Phenotypic
        Transition of Macrophages. Planta Med 2019;85:563–9.
[145]   Phetcharat L, Wongsuphasawat K, Winther K. The effectiveness of
        a standardized rose hip powder, containing seeds and shells of Rosa
        canina, on cell longevity, skin wrinkles, moisture, and elasticity. Clin
        Interv Aging 2015;19:1849–56.
[146]   Lin T-K, Zhong L, Santiago, Luis J. Anti-Inflammatory and Skin
        Barrier Repair Effects of Topical Application of Some Plant Oils.

Int J Mol Sci 2017;19:70.

[147] Therapeutic Research Faculty. Rose Hip. WebMD 2020. https://www.webmd.com/vitamins/ai/ingredientmono-839/rose-hip.

[148] Duxbury J. Rosehip soup - Nyponsoppa. SwedishFood 2021. https://www.swedishfood.com/swedish-food-recipes-desserts/217-rose hip-soup.

[149] Jönsson J. Nyponsoppa. Wikimedia Commons 2009. https://commons.wikimedia.org/wiki/File:Nyponsoppa.jpg.

[150] GERARD J. The Herball, or, Generall historie of plantes. 1636.

[151] Salo A. Vaccinium myrtillus Mustikka. Wikimedia Commons 2011. https://commons.wikimedia.org/wiki/File:Vaccinium_myrtillus_M ustikka_IMG_1100_C-_cropped.jpg.

[152] Wikipedia. Vaccinium vitis-idaea. Wikipedia 2021. https://en.wikipedia.org/wiki/Vaccinium_vitis-idaea.

[153] Patel CA, Divakar K, Santani D, Solanki HK, Thakkar JH. Remedial Prospective of Hippophae rhamnoides Linn. (Sea Buckthorn). ISRN Pharmacol 2012.

[154] Mikstas C. Sea Buckthorn. WebMD 2021. https://www.webmd.com/vitamins-and-supplements/sea-buckthorn-uses-and-risks.

[155] Johansson AK, Korte H, Yang B, Stanley JC, Kallio PH. Sea buckthorn berry oil inhibits platelet aggregation. J Nutr Biochem 2000;11:491–5.

[156] Gao S, Guo Q, Qin C, Shang R, Zhang Z. Sea Buckthorn Fruit Oil Extract Alleviates Insulin Resistance through the PI3K/Akt Signaling Pathway in Type 2 Diabetes Mellitus Cells and Rats. J Agric Food Chem 2017;65:1328–36.

[157] Gupta A, Kumar R, Pal K, Singh V, Banerjee PK, Sawhney RC. Influence of sea buckthorn (Hippophae rhamnoides L.) flavone on dermal wound healing in rats. Mol Celluar Biochem 2006;193:1–2.

[158] Naveed A, Braga V. Anti-Aging Effects of Hippophae rhamnoides Emulsion on Human Skin. Trop J Pharm Res 2012;12.

[159] Russo M, Spagnuolo C, Tedesco I, Bilotto S, Russo GL. The flavonoid quercetin in disease prevention and therapy: facts and fancies. Biochem Pharmacol 2012;83:6–15.

[160] Guan M, Zhou Y, Zhu Q-L, Liu Y, Bei Y-Y, Zhang X-N, et al. N-trimethyl chitosan nanoparticle-encapsulated lactosyl-norcantharidin for liver cancer therapy with high targeting efficacy. Nanomedicine Nanotechnology, Biol Med 2012;8:1172–81.

ABOUT THE AUTHORS

Husband and Wife RHP and Hagen Wiking, along with our young son, have a passion for all things health, nutrition, cooking, history, and Scandinavia. We sincerely thank you for taking the time to read this book, and hope you not only learned a few things, but were also entertained while doing so.

Made in the USA
Las Vegas, NV
02 November 2023

80131660R00095